Wh

to Speak Your
Mind

Political protests, debates on college campuses, and social media tirades make it seem like everyone is speaking their minds today. Surveys, however, reveal that many people increasingly feel like they're walking on eggshells when communicating in public. Speaking your mind can risk relationships and professional opportunities. It can alienate friends and anger colleagues. Isn't it smarter to just put your head down and keep quiet about controversial topics?

In this book, Hrishikesh Joshi offers a novel defense of speaking your mind. He explains that because we are social creatures, we never truly think alone. What we know depends on what our community knows. And by bringing our unique perspectives to bear upon public discourse, we enhance our collective ability to reach the truth on a variety of important matters.

Speaking your mind is also important for your own sake. It is essential for developing your own thinking. And it's a core aspect of being intellectually courageous and independent. Joshi argues that such independence is a crucial part of a well-lived life.

The book draws from Aristotle, John Stuart Mill, Friedrich Nietzsche, Bertrand Russell, and a range of contemporary thinkers to argue that it's OK to speak your mind.

Hrishikesh Joshi is Assistant Professor at Bowling Green State University, and works on moral and political philosophy. He completed his Ph.D. at Princeton University.

Why It's OK: The Ethics and Aesthetics of
How We Live

ABOUT THE SERIES:

Philosophers often build cogent arguments for unpopular
positions. Recent examples include cases against marriage and
pregnancy, for treating animals as our equals, and dismissing
some popular art as aesthetically inferior. What philosophers
have done less often is to offer compelling arguments for
widespread and established human behavior, like getting
married, having children, eating animals, and going to the
movies. But if one role for philosophy is to help us reflect
on our lives and build sound justifications for our beliefs
and actions, it seems odd that philosophers would neglect
arguments for the lifestyles most people—including many
philosophers—actually lead. Unfortunately, philosophers'
inattention to normalcy has meant that the ways of life that
define our modern societies have gone largely without defense,
even as whole literatures have emerged to condemn them.

Why It's OK: The Ethics and Aesthetics of How We Live seeks
to remedy that. It's a series of books that provides accessible,
sound, and often new and creative arguments for widespread
ethical and aesthetic values. Made up of short volumes that
assume no previous knowledge of philosophy from the reader,
the series recognizes that philosophy is just as important for
understanding what we already believe as it is for criticizing
the status quo. The series isn't meant to make us complacent
about what we value; rather, it helps and challenges us to think
more deeply about the values that give our daily lives meaning.

Titles in Series:

Why It's OK to Want to Be Rich

Jason Brennan

Why It's OK to Be of Two Minds

Jennifer Church

Why It's OK to Ignore Politics

Christopher Freiman

Why It's OK to Make Bad Choices

William Glod

Why It's OK to Enjoy the Work of Immoral Artists

Mary Beth Willard

Why It's OK to Speak Your Mind

Hrishikesh Joshi

Selected Forthcoming Titles:

Why It's OK to Get Married

Christie J. Hartley

Why It's OK to Love Bad Movies

Matthew Strohl

Why It's OK to Eat Meat

Dan C. Shahar

Why It's OK to Mind Your Own Business

Justin Tosi and Brandon Warmke

Why It's OK to Be Fat

Rekha Nath

Why It's OK to Be a Moral Failure

Robert Talisse

For further information about this series, please visit: www.routledge.com/
Why-Its-OK/book-series/WIOK

HRISHIKESH JOSHI

Why It's OK to Speak Your Mind

Routledge
Taylor & Francis Group
NEW YORK AND LONDON

First published 2021
by Routledge
52 Vanderbilt Avenue, New York, NY 10017

and by Routledge
2 Park Square, Milton Park, Abingdon, Oxon, OX14 4RN

Routledge is an imprint of the Taylor & Francis Group, an informa business

© 2021 Taylor & Francis

The right of Hrishikesh Joshi to be identified as author of this work has been asserted by him in accordance with sections 77 and 78 of the Copyright, Designs and Patents Act 1988.

Library of Congress Cataloging-in-Publication Data
A catalog record for this title has been requested

ISBN: 978-0-367-14171-4 (hbk)
ISBN: 978-0-367-14172-1 (pbk)
ISBN: 978-1-003-14575-2 (ebk)

Typeset in Joanna MT Pro and DIN pro
by Apex CoVantage, LLC

MIX
Paper from
responsible sources
FSC® C013985

Printed in the United Kingdom
by Henry Ling Limited

Let us speak of this, you who are wisest, even if it be bad. Silence is worse; all truths that are kept silent become poisonous.

—Friedrich Nietzsche, *Thus Spoke Zarathustra*

Contents

Contents

Acknowledgments

My path towards writing this book was tortuous. The predicament was that I was supposed to do engineering, but was born to do philosophy. When I came across a collection of philosophical essays at the local library in Nevis, I was immediately drawn to the questions and the methods. I began to read Descartes, Spinoza, and Plato, among others, and began to write down my reactions to their ideas. But the social expectation was that I would study engineering (or medicine, or something like that), so as to have a stable career.

I thought I could work on philosophy on the side, but eventually realized that this is not really possible in the 21st century. In 2008, after much painstaking deliberation, I quit a Ph.D. program in engineering to begin afresh in philosophy. I moved back to Los Angeles, to take some courses at the University of Southern California, my alma mater, to see if I could become an academic philosopher.

It was a big gamble, but I was fortunate to meet great mentors. At USC, Scott Soames and Gary Watson were enormously encouraging and nurturing. Without Scott's support in particular, I wouldn't be where I am. In 2010, the stars somehow aligned and I was admitted to the graduate philosophy program at Princeton University. Throughout my time there, Gideon Rosen, Michael Smith, and Philip Pettit were patient and extremely generous advisors. Daniel Jacobson, then at the

University of Michigan, gave me my first job in the field, and I worked closely with him for two years in Ann Arbor. Dan always gave rigorous feedback, while at the same time encouraging me to develop my ideas.

The process of writing this book has benefitted tremendously from the input of many friends and colleagues. I owe a special debt of gratitude to Daniel Greco, Yoaav Isaacs, J.P. Messina, Noel Swanson, and Daniel Wolt, who commented in detail on early drafts of the manuscript. I am also thankful to Pranav Ambardekar, Spencer Case, Daniel Demetriou, Ada Fee, Jason Iuliano, Madison Kilbride, Kristin Mickelson, Oliver Traldi, and Kevin Vallier for helpful discussion of the main arguments presented here. Andrew Huddleston, Nadeem Hussain, and Timothy Stoll gave extremely valuable comments on the chapter drawing on Nietzsche.

I have been thinking about the subject matter of this book for several years. But the project took concrete shape after Andy Beck from Routledge got in touch with me in 2018 about a new series he was developing. I thought it was a great idea and drew up a proposal. Throughout the process, Andy has been very helpful. The book has also benefitted from excellent referee comments during both review stages. Most of the manuscript itself was written in the summer of 2020. During this time, I was supported in part via a research grant from the Institute for Humane Studies. This aided me in putting my full focus on the project.

Finally, I owe serious thanks to Meghan Gottschall for reading multiple drafts of this book and to Meghan, Henry, and Freddy for putting up with me as I was writing it.

Speaking your mind can have consequences. We constantly face pressures to conform to the opinions—or at least *perceived* opinions—of our peers, friends, and employers. Dissenting from these views can have real costs. Often, the best way to advance in one's career, for example, will involve not "rocking the boat" too much. Saying what you really believe might come at the cost of lost job opportunities, promotions—and in more extreme, but nowadays not uncommon, cases, getting fired.

What's more, these sorts of pressures exist in their strongest form precisely within those professions and institutions which are primarily responsible for producing new ideas, maintaining the stock of knowledge, and shaping culture. Dissent from the zeitgeist of the cultural elite is less likely to be the cause of lost employment for truckers, plumbers, or mining engineers. It's much more of an issue for writers, journalists, academics, and artists. But if such pressures exist most strongly within these professions, and if such pressures can cause group-think and blind spots, then it seems particularly important to address them because of the power such professions have in determining public opinion.

Now, of course, legal sanctions for the expression of ideas are rare within modern democracies. The United States has protections built in to the Constitution itself, in the form of the First Amendment. You cannot go to jail for merely voicing an opinion—no matter how heterodox or repulsive. But this protection is nowhere near enough to safeguard our collective ability to evade the perils of conformity. John Stuart Mill, perhaps the most preeminent historical defender of free expression, was acutely aware of this issue. He wrote:

> In respect to all persons but those whose pecuniary circumstances make them independent of the goodwill of other people, opinion, on this subject, is as efficacious as law; men might as well be imprisoned, as excluded from the means of earning their bread.[1]

Bertrand Russell, one of the premier analytic philosophers of the 20th century and a defender of liberalism, echoed this idea decades later:

> Legal penalties are, however, in the modern world, the least of the obstacles to freedom of thought. The two great obstacles are economic penalties and distortion of evidence. It is clear that thought is not free if the profession of certain opinions makes it impossible to earn a living. It is clear also that thought is not free if all the arguments on one side of a controversy are perpetually presented as attractively as possible, while the arguments on the other side can only be discovered by diligent search.[2]

Unless you are independently wealthy, the costs of self-expression can be very real despite the legal protections. Even if you are wealthy, there are substantial risks associated with saying what you think about contentious topics. For one, there can be reputational costs—from friends, neighbors, or colleagues. And bad reputations, even if unfounded, have tendencies to stick. In addition, if you stray too far from sanctioned opinion, you may eventually lose access to the very means of expressing your opinions to the broader public: op-eds or TV appearances, for example. That said, the democratization of information dissemination via the internet has in some ways reduced the power of gatekeeper institutions in this regard—though not entirely, because the internet has gatekeeper institutions of its own.

Given that speaking your mind has costs, what should you do?

This question is increasingly relevant for the many who feel that they often can't say what they really think. This is the question I want to explore. What this book is *not* trying to do is to defend, in the first instance, the ideal of free speech—that is, the notion that society and its institutions should be open to dissenting opinion. If you want a defense of *that* idea, you can do no better than to read John Stuart Mill's *On Liberty*, particularly Chapter 2.

Rather, what I want to do here is to defend the idea that we often have a duty to speak our minds, even in the face of the sorts of costs mentioned above. And furthermore, a good life involves the cultivation of intellectual independence, which we cannot achieve without the outward expression of our ideas. A life of intellectual conformity and status seeking, I will argue, leaves something important to be desired.

Below is a quick bird's-eye view of the main arguments of this book.

SYNOPSIS

Speaking our minds, against social pressure not to do so, can often help improve the condition of what I will call the "epistemic commons"—that is, the stock of evidence, ideas, and perspectives that are alive for a given community. This is because our knowledge is essentially *distributed*, due to the division of cognitive labor. We are deeply reliant on others for what we take ourselves to know. Few of us actually know how a zipper works, for example, but we often take ourselves to know this because we can easily access the relevant facts. In this way, we do not and cannot think alone.

This is in many ways an indispensable blessing: imagine having to figure out everything by yourself! Yet it is also a curse. As the ocean is vulnerable to overfishing and the atmosphere is vulnerable to pollution, the epistemic commons is vulnerable to *social pressure*. Social pressure can distort our picture of the world, often dangerously. And if we have a distorted view of what the world is like, then the actions we take can be counterproductive—even if our intentions are good.

The handling of the Chernobyl nuclear disaster in the former Soviet Union is a prime example of evidence distortion leading to catastrophe. Much of the disaster could have been averted had the authorities and the general public a better idea of what was going on. But because evidence was suppressed at crucial junctures, the response to the disaster allowed for many more deaths than it had to.

While the Chernobyl disaster occurred under an authoritarian government, democracies are not immune to the underlying phenomenon. Social pressure can cause evidence to pile up on one side of a debate or issue, while evidence on the other side is systematically screened out. A person who looks at the evidence as it is presented, then, will form a warped view of the matter, even if she rationally evaluates the evidence at hand. I will suggest that whenever there exists social pressure to conceal evidence on one side of a topic, we should suspect that a (possibly dangerous) blind spot is lurking somewhere, due to this mechanism. The catch, and it is a big catch, is that the blind spot will not be recognizable by people who simply look at the evidence as it is presented. They will be unaware that their view of the world is distorted.

We should be especially mindful of social pressure in those institutions most closely associated with knowledge production and dissemination: particularly universities, but also thinktanks, newspapers, and so on. In contexts where there is social pressure within a community not to give evidence for certain conclusions, the output of that community cannot be taken seriously—or at least it must be taken with a generous serving of salt. Nonetheless, the danger is for outsiders to take this output at face value: through no fault of their own, they might be unaware of the social pressures within the community. This is our modern epistemic predicament, though it has received little recent philosophical attention.

Given these dynamics, I will suggest there is a duty to reveal our evidence against the social pressure, so long as the costs are not too high. In this sense, you have a duty to speak your mind against social pressure, at least some of the time. The duty is imperfect in the sense that we can pick our battles. We don't have to speak our minds in every single context; that would be too onerous and generally unwise. Nonetheless, there is a duty to speak up against social pressure because this constitutes doing your part to protect a common resource—namely, the epistemic commons. Someone who never does this is a free rider. He benefits from the work of others but never does his part to contribute—much like the roommate who never does dishes or the dog walker who never picks up after the dog.

If you work in one of the institutions of knowledge production mentioned earlier, one way you can significantly benefit humanity's epistemic position is by pursuing heterodox projects. The marginal value of this type of work is very high. The first article defending X or developing a new way of seeing things is vastly more valuable than the 1000th article defending not-X or making a small move in some arcane debate. Those with the protection of tenure are in an especially good position to do this and to help others who are pursuing such work.

Now, the structure of the free riding problem identified here creates a worry that many readers will share. Given the many actors involved in the maintenance of the epistemic commons (think of all the people who drive science or a particular culture), we might wonder if our individual actions make a real difference. Climate change seems to be a case like this. What difference will it make if *you* stop eating hamburgers? Probably not much, given the scope of the problem. But isn't speaking your mind like this? What difference can one person make?

Quite a lot, it turns out. Even *one* dissenter can have a huge psychological impact on others. This is borne out in several psychological studies, most notably the famous Solomon Asch experiments. One person calling it like they see it can relieve the fear of isolation that other potential dissenters might be experiencing. That person can be you. This is also a lesson we can draw from Hans Christian Andersen's fairy tale "The Emperor's New Clothes"—when the child points out that the emperor has no clothes, everyone suddenly musters the courage to say it themselves. In this way, a lone voice can burst the bubble of what social scientists call "pluralistic ignorance," which is a situation wherein most people think something but are unaware that they are in the majority.

Speaking your mind for the sake of the *common good* is the subject matter of Chapters 1–3. Chapters 4 and 5 contend that you should speak your mind *for your own sake*. Speaking your mind is an essential component of the good life. Or so I will argue.

The question of what makes for a good life has been a core preoccupation of philosophers for as long as there has been philosophy. When we look at a life as a whole, under what conditions might we say: "this here was a life well-lived"? Two natural answers present themselves immediately: pleasure and social status. According to the first option, a life goes well for the person who lives it to the extent that it contains lots of pleasure (which encompasses not only things like gustatory and sexual pleasure, but also feelings of contentment, satisfaction, and the like) and little pain (physical pain, but also frustration, depression, etc.) The second option is that a good life contains lots of social status: thus, CEOs, presidents, deans, Nobel Prize winners, musical celebrities, etc., are living the best lives.

The great ancient Greek philosophers considered these two answers and found them wanting. For Aristotle, what makes something—anything—good is whether it fulfills its characteristic work (*ergon*) well. Therefore, if we want to know what a good human life is, we need to think about what is the characteristic work of humans. In other words, what is distinctive about humans *qua* humans? Aristotle thought it is our capacity to *reason*. Hence, he thought the good human life is one that exhibits the proper development and exercise of reason.

Recent work in philosophy and psychology suggests we simply cannot reason well in isolation. In order to reason well, we must find interlocutors with whom we can go back and forth. Reasoning is an *essentially social* activity. But if that's right, then reasoning well involves speaking your mind, rather than keeping all your distinctive thoughts and ideas to yourself. Aristotle's teacher's teacher, Socrates, was a living embodiment of this ideal. He roamed Athens challenging the cherished assumptions of his fellow Athenians. For this, he was put to death by a jury. But even then, he had no regrets. From his perspective, the unexamined life was not worth living anyway. Now, this may well be a bit much, but if these ideas have something to them, then at the very least we should not sacrifice our integrity as thinkers willy-nilly for accolades and prestige and approval.

A somewhat different strand of thinking about the good life emphasizes *independence*. Great human lives do something unique, create something new, and refuse to follow the cultural zeitgeist everywhere it goes. This is a major theme for the 19th century philosophers John Stuart Mill and Friedrich Nietzsche. Their ideas are of deep relevance to thinking about the pressures to conform that we experience today, and might help to put these pressures into broader ethical perspective. Many of the trends they identified in their own time seem to exist in an even stronger and more potent form in the 21st century. Hence, revisiting their works, not merely as historical curiosities, but as offering perspectives worth engaging with and drawing from, can greatly benefit us with respect to our current predicaments.

Importantly, for our purposes, the independence they extol cannot be cultivated if we never speak our minds: because we are fundamentally *social* creatures, we must express and exchange our ideas and values outwardly in order to be genuinely independent.

The book ends with an exploration of how the future of humanity is a condition of many things mattering to us here and now. Philosopher Samuel Scheffler has recently presented novel arguments for this idea. According to him, much of what we value here and now assumes a future for humanity; without such an assurance, we would be gripped by nihilism and despair. This is just part of the picture, however; I argue that we don't just want humanity to continue but also to *flourish*. But if social pressures can create dangerous blind spots, then given the speed at which modern life is evolving, it seems all the more important to speak our minds so as to combat these blind spots. There is far too much at stake, given what we care about.

One

Madness is rare in individuals—but in groups, political parties, nations, and eras it is the rule.

—Friedrich Nietzsche, *Beyond Good and Evil*

Every age has its peculiar folly; some scheme, project, or phantasy into which it plunges, spurred on either by the love of gain, the necessity of excitement, or the mere force of imitation. Failing in these, it has some madness, to which it is goaded by political or religious causes, or both combined.

—Charles Mackay, *Extraordinary Popular Delusions and the Madness of Crowds*

THE DIVISION OF COGNITIVE LABOR

Modern society is only possible because of the division of labor. Without division of labor, the most we could achieve is a very meager standard of living. Imagine you had to make everything you use, by yourself, from scratch—without tools created by others, without water and food provided by others, without medicines invented by others. Most of us would not survive for a month, if that. Division of labor makes modern standards of living possible because with individuals specializing in one area, society as a whole is able to be much more productive.

Adam Smith illustrated and developed this idea in his *Wealth of Nations* by using the example of a pin factory. Imagine ten people tasked with making pins. If each person had to make a whole pin, perhaps each might make ten pins a day. Making a whole pin involves several distinct processes. Let's suppose it involves ten different tasks. Well, if one person had to do all these tasks we can expect that there would be time lost as that person transitioned from one task to another. Furthermore, it would be hard to become skilled at all these different tasks—that would require lots of training and effort. But what if each person in the factory focused on just one of the ten tasks instead? Time would be saved in a myriad of ways, and the factory would be able to produce a lot more pins—though, no person by himself would be making a whole pin. As a result, the factory might produce 10,000 pins total per day, whereas it would have produced only 100 without specialization. Modern society is like this pin factory writ large.[1]

But division of labor in modern life is not limited to the production of physical goods. The other face of specialization is the division of *cognitive* labor. Our institutions of knowledge production (universities, thinktanks, private research labs) reflect this feature: researchers inevitably specialize in one tiny sub-sub-field or two in order to make new discoveries. Yet, the division of cognitive labor has deep implications. What we are able to know is inextricably tied to what I will call the *epistemic commons*—the stock of facts, ideas, and perspectives that are alive in society's discourse.

In their book, *The Knowledge Illusion*, cognitive scientists Steven Sloman and Philip Fernbach write: "Language, memory, attention—indeed, all mental functions—can be thought of as operating in a way that is distributed across a community according to a division of cognitive labor."[2] The authors argue that we know very little, but take ourselves to know a lot because the relevant facts are easily accessible to us. If Sloman and

Fernbach are right, then our epistemic health as individuals—i.e. the extent to which our beliefs accurately represent the world—is inextricably tied to the health of the epistemic commons.

Consider the following. Do you understand how a zipper works? How about a flush toilet? These objects seem basic enough. Knowing how they work isn't exactly rocket science. But people drastically overestimate their understanding of how these simple items function. In one study, Leon Rozenblit and Frank Keil asked people to rate from one to seven how well they understood the workings of such objects. They then asked participants to actually explain in detail how the objects worked. Many were simply unable to do so. And so when asked to revisit the question of how well they understood, subjects drastically lowered their ratings. Psychologist Rebecca Lawson performed a similar experiment where students were asked to explain, by sketching out the mechanism, how a bicycle works. The results were striking—most people were unable to complete the task, even though a bicycle is such a familiar object in our daily lives. This phenomenon, of people thinking they know much more than they actually do, has come to be known as the illusion of explanatory depth.[3]

Why might we fall prey to this illusion? Well for one, the relevant information is easily accessible. If you want to know how a zipper really works, a simple internet search will give you all the details you need. Though you may not actually as of this moment know the workings of a zipper, the knowledge is "at your fingertips," as it were. What this suggests is our representation of the world is like a low-resolution map such that "zooming in" only gives a clear picture insofar as we are able to rely upon the knowledge others have. With respect to most areas of the map, we are unable to zoom in by ourselves—and if we do, we'll just see large pixels that don't look like anything. The division of cognitive labor, then, renders our epistemic lives intricately tied with the efforts and contributions of others.

Furthermore, the very coarse-grained picture we have of the world will itself depend on which perspectives are "alive" in the discourse within our milieu. Consider, for example, a teenager within a deeply religious sect living in a small village. Suppose that this sect does not believe in Darwinian evolution. The arguments for evolution are not discussed, and when the topic is broached, people quickly dismiss it as an unsubstantiated theory. Some might raise what they take to be decisive counterarguments like: "How come we don't see monkeys turning into humans now?" or "Where are the missing links?" and so on. Now the teenager might be able, in principle, to discover the powerful arguments in favor of evolution by natural selection. There is a copy of the *Origin of Species* at the local library, and she could also spend time delving into encyclopedias and biology textbooks. But for all intents and purposes, her map of the world has a large hole in it. What's more, given that there are ample other constraints on her time, she might simply not find it worthwhile inquiring further.

In this way, there are lots of questions that we might lack the time or imagination to inquire about if the people we're surrounded by consider the issue settled. Division of cognitive labor means we simply cannot independently verify all the claims we take for granted. But that in turn means that if the view our community settles on is mistaken or impoverished, the distortion easily transfers to us. Our epistemic health thus depends on the epistemic health of our milieu.

The 19th century mathematician and philosopher W.K. Clifford underscored this social, interconnected nature of our ability to understand and describe the world in his landmark essay on the ethics of belief:

> Our lives are guided by that general conception of the course of things which has been created by society for social purposes. Our words, our phrases, our forms and processes and modes of thought, are common property, fashioned and perfected from age to age; an heirloom which every succeeding generation inherits as a precious deposit and a sacred trust to be handed on to the next one, not unchanged but enlarged and purified, with some clear marks of its proper handiwork. Into this, for good or ill, is woven every belief of every man who has speech of his fellows. An awful privilege, and an awful responsibility, that we should help to create the world in which posterity will live.[4]

For Clifford, this meant that each of us has an important ethical responsibility: namely, to believe only on the basis of proper evidence. As I will be arguing in the next chapter, if our epistemic situation is a common resource in this way, then we all have a duty to do what we can to preserve the integrity of this resource. However, believing on the basis of proper evidence, though important in its own right, is *not enough*—we also have a duty to speak our minds.

BLIND SPOTS AND SOCIAL PRESSURE

To set the stage for that argument, it is necessary to examine the way in which the epistemic commons is vulnerable. Tragedies of the commons arise because common resources are often susceptible to damage and degradation.[5] For example, industrial pollution can destroy river ecosystems. Analogously, I will argue below, *social pressure* can degrade the epistemic commons.

Consider again the village described above. Why might reasons to accept evolution be systematically repressed here? Presumably because publicly defending such reasons will come at some cost to one's social status, the maintenance of which is a strong motivation for most people.[6] Somebody discussing evidence in favor of Darwinian evolution might be seen as deviant, and perhaps not a true believer of the religion. Furthermore, accusations of heresy or disbelief can invite severe repercussions in many deeply religious societies—even if such accusations end up being untrue. Thus, even if somebody were to encounter or think of a reason to believe in evolution, they might keep that thought to themselves, especially if they're unsure of the soundness of the reason. Why risk your reputation and social standing (or worse, in many places and times) just to voice some reason you're unsure of?

In this way, social pressure can systematically filter out reasons to believe a particular claim. The reasons that don't get filtered out will make it look like that claim ought to be rejected—even if had there been no such filtering, then people would be justified in believing the claim. In other words, filtering processes created by social pressure allow reasons to pile up on one side of an argument while those on the other side get discarded. Yet, the overall balance of reasons, had open discourse prevailed, might well have supported the other side. Any time we observe social pressure to avoid giving some kinds of reasons, then, we should suspect that a worrisome blind spot exists in some form or another.

Importantly, we can't dismiss the existence of such distortions simply by surveying the first-order evidence (i.e. evidence directly relevant to the issue at hand) presented to us. The problem is created precisely because evidence is filtered in such a way as to support one conclusion. It's then no good to simply look at the evidence that is presented and say: "but the conclusion is obviously right!" The conclusion *looks* obviously right because countervailing evidence is not allowed to surface and accumulate, due to the presence of social pressure. A collective blind spot can exist in this way even if the members of a community *respond rationally* to the first-order evidence they have.

A DETAILED EXAMPLE: THREE ENGINEERS AND A DAM

Consider the following example. Imagine a situation where three engineers are responsible for the construction and upkeep of a particular dam. Suppose that constructing the dam has been a project that has required enormous funding and mobilization of resources. Imagine also that the dam has an enormous positive impact on the livelihoods of the surrounding community—it provides essential power and irrigation. So, naturally, the community as a whole has a strong interest in the success of the project. Besides, the dam construction is a big feather in the cap for many local officials and politicians. People want to believe it will succeed, and opponents of the project as well as doubters are not looked upon favorably.

Now, a dam bursting, of course, can be really devastating. Suppose there are some good reasons to think that this particular dam will hold during this particular year. But there are also reasons to think the dam will break. The reasons to think the dam will hold are common knowledge among the engineers, since there's no social pressure not to voice these reasons. However, the reasons to think the dam will break are distributed among the engineers. They keep these reasons to themselves because they don't want to be seen as naysayers.

Suppose that the reasons to think the dam will break outweigh the reasons to think the dam will hold. Basically, given the total evidence, the dam is going to break. The resulting case has the following feature: it would be rational *given the evidence of the group as a whole* to believe the dam will break. Yet it is not true of *any particular individual* that she should believe the dam will break given the evidence she has.

To fix ideas, suppose the following are the relevant considerations ('R' for 'reason').

Pro:

R_1 = the dam is constructed with good materials.
R_2 = the structural engineering is sound overall.

Con:

R_3 = the upstream rainfall has been unusually high this year.
R_4 = the spillway design has some defects.
R_5 = the outlet pipe maintenance has been suboptimal.

None of the con considerations is by itself sufficient evidence to think the dam will break, given the pro reasons. However, the considerations taken as a whole—i.e. R_1 through R_5—support the conclusion that the dam will break. But now suppose that each of the three engineers knows both R_1 and R_2 (since there's no social pressure to hide these) but only *one* of the remaining reasons.

So, suppose the first engineer knows R_1, R_2, and R_3, the second knows R_1, R_2, and R_4, and the third knows R_1, R_2, and R_5. Each engineer believes the dam will not break—and given the evidence each has, this is indeed the rational conclusion for each to draw. But the *group as a whole* is irrational in a sense. For the group as a whole is in possession of evidence such that it would be rational to believe the dam will break, and therefore to take steps to fix it if possible or to evacuate the surrounding population.[7]

Why might each engineer not reveal her counterevidence? Well she might think something like this: "I have some evidence to think the dam will be in trouble, but the overall case for the integrity of the dam is really strong. If I raise concerns about the dam, all that will happen is I will invite social opprobrium. Nothing good will come out of it, because given what I know, the dam is not going to break anyway." So, in other words, there's a downside but there's no upside.

Notice that such silence need not be borne out of pure selfishness. It need not be the case that the engineers only care about themselves and not the people who would be affected were the dam to break. We can even suppose that if the dam breaks, all three of the engineers' houses will get destroyed. So, if any of these engineers *knew* the rest of the evidence, let's suppose they'd bring it to the attention of the others, despite the risk of social opprobrium. I'll risk some flak if it means saving thousands of lives, including my house, they might think. But the issue is that none of them is in a position to know that the dam will break *because* they act in a way that's rational given what they know. In this way social pressure can blind us to what the right course of action is, given what our group as a whole knows.

LESSONS FROM THE 20TH CENTURY

Evidential situations like these can lead to catastrophe. If information is not freely shared within a group due to social pressure, deliberation on very important issues can be distorted. In the above case, the dam will break and ruin many lives.

Moreover, this is not simply an exercise of the imagination. Many avoidable disasters have occurred because there was pressure not to share certain kinds of information. The Chernobyl disaster, in which a nuclear powerplant malfunctioned and exploded in what is modern-day Ukraine, is perhaps a paradigm example. Due to the authoritarian, top-down government in place at the time, individuals had incentives not to raise alarms about radiation levels, the nature of the explosion, substandard materials, etc. The result was devastating for thousands of people, many of whom continue to feel the effects of radiation poisoning to this day. The HBO series *Chernobyl* offers a detailed look at the deliberations and actions of various individuals as they grappled with the situation in a way that brings out the incentives they had to distort or suppress information.[8]

Democracies typically do a better job of avoiding unnecessary disasters and missteps like this. The victory of the Allies in World War II can be partly attributed to the nature of information flow within democratic decision-making.[9] In the democracies, members of the army were relatively more able and willing to offer information that would lead to course-correction by the upper chain of command. By contrast, within the German army and air force, people were much more hesitant about displeasing their superior officers with news or information or strategic perspectives that might be seen to dampen the war effort.

Democracies are also able to allow the spread of key information through a more open media. Journalists are less prone to intimidation by the government, and thus can quickly disseminate crucial news to civilians and government officials alike. Luther Gulick, who served as a high-level American official during World War II, explained that in contrast, decisions within authoritarian governments are "hatched in secret by a small group of partially informed men and then enforced through dictatorial authority."[10] Democracies are thus able to avoid some of the epistemic pitfalls that beset authoritarian regimes because the channels of information are much freer.

This is no cause for complacency, however. Democracies are not immune to such problems. For example, the infamous Bay of Pigs fiasco a failed U.S.-backed landing attempt on Cuba in 1961, resulted in part because those who had doubts about the plan suppressed their reservations.[11] Moreover, social pressure need not always come from government authorities. Think of college students who feel pressure to binge drink, the many of us who feel pressure to dress in particular ways, teenagers who (used to) feel pressure to smoke cigarettes—or, what's more relevant here, people who feel pressure not to publicly express certain social or political opinions. Such forms of social pressure do not come top-down, from some governmental chain of command. Rather, they are much more spontaneous and organic. These pressures *emerge* from the incentives, interactions, and choices of millions of people who shape a particular culture. Democracy, then, does not solve all the informational problems systemic within authoritarian regimes.

THE IMPORTANCE OF REFERENCE NETWORKS

Which pressures to conform we experience depends crucially on our *reference networks*. Philosopher Cristina Bicchieri, known for her work on social norms, uses the concept to illustrate that the set of people who matter when it comes to influencing your norm-guided behavior is not always the set physically closest to you. Thus, a religious, married Mormon individual's reference network might centrally involve her religious family and other Mormon friends rather than the atheist singles living in her city, who may be physically closer to her. An academic's reference network may largely consist of other academics even if he lives in a neighborhood comprised mostly of blue-collar families.

The cultures that have the greatest impact on us, then, are not necessarily those most physically close to us. And they may be cultures associated with a minority of the population, as in the Mormon example above. It's not always a matter of similar demographics either. For instance, according to Bicchieri, "A young woman in Philadelphia wearing very high heels will probably not care what other women do in India, or even New Orleans. Her reference network may be the 'fashionable' crowd in her town, those who she is likely to meet and give her a chance to 'show off,' or it may be a celebrity, magazine starlets, or TV series that girls in her reference network follow."[12]

Now the pattern I have been describing—where the evidence on one side is common knowledge but the evidence on the other side is distributed and isolated—has important epistemic and ethical implications which have received little philosophical attention. The pattern may explain some of the phenomena we observe in public discourse and public opinion—in particular, how political polarization on a range of separate issues can be maintained. Crucial to the analysis is a characterization of the social pressures and information channels within people's reference networks.

Consider a person, Alice, whose reference network consists mostly of supporters of one party. Now imagine that Alice agrees with her reference network, given her analysis of the information she has, on all but one issue. Let's say that on this particular issue, she has some pretty strong evidence. Suppose this issue has to do with the causes of, and effective methods of reducing, violent crime. Alice has done a deep dive into the available data on crime and policing, and is statistically savvy enough to draw reasonable conclusions. Now, Alice disagrees with her group on this issue, but the evidence she has is strong enough that many others in her group, if they deliberate rationally with this evidence in hand, will come to change their views on the topic.

Nonetheless, Alice may not share this evidence with her group. For one, she might be keenly aware of the flak she will receive if she disagrees with her reference network on an issue of contentious partisan disagreement. Even if she doesn't explicitly lose friends, people may look upon her with more suspicion. She might also lose out on future professional opportunities if she signals to others that she's not a good member of the ideological group. So that's the downside. What's the upside? Well, by Alice's own lights, her group gets things mostly right anyway. Sharing the evidence that she has will only empower the other group relative to her group, which will be, on balance, counterproductive from her perspective. Thus, the rational thing to do is to keep that evidence to herself.

But now note that Alice may not be the only one facing such a situation. Imagine that Bob, another member of the group, disagrees on the issue of the minimum wage. He has good evidence that would suggest a position contrary to the group's accepted wisdom. But he agrees with the group on all the other issues, including crime and policing. Claire might disagree with the group's position on abortion, having thought a lot about the topic and delved into the arguments on both sides of the debate. However, she agrees with the group on all the other topics, including crime and policing as well as the minimum wage.

The dissenters don't share their evidence. However, *were* the evidence to be shared, the group's overall position on a variety of partisan issues may well be dramatically undermined. This fact, however, will not be transparent to the members of the group. Given what first-order evidence they have, it makes sense for them to think their group is right on the whole.

This dynamic may be a good explanation of the pattern of polarization we observe in modern life. We find public opinion divided strongly along partisan lines, but on issues that seem to be rationally disconnected. For example, particular positions on gun control, criminal justice, immigration, climate change, abortion, minimum wage, and a host of other issues travel together. In other words, if you pick a person at random and all you know about them is their view on gun control and climate change, you can probably predict their opinion with good accuracy on abortion and immigration. But why should this be so? It would seem that these issues have nothing to do with each other—a particular position on gun control shouldn't commit you to any view on abortion or minimum wage. To put it another way: the set of considerations, statistics, and arguments relevant to each of these issues is quite distinct. So, what explains this pattern? Partisans of either side, of course, will be tempted to say the other side is simply wrong about every issue at hand. And they'll point to the first-order evidence they have on a variety of issues, which supports the views of their side, and thus implies that the other side's views are wrong.

But what could possibly *explain why* the other side would get everything wrong and one's own side would get everything right? There are a variety of flat-footed responses partisans will be tempted to give: the other side is dumb, brainwashed, evil, selfish, and so on. These responses, however satisfying from the point of view of the partisan, are challenging to sustain.[13] It is also worth exploring non-cynical hypotheses that could show how generally well-meaning individuals come to form their beliefs on contentious issues. What is needed here is a way of explaining how people seem to come to accept one of two packages of disconnected beliefs. The model formulated above, of social pressure acting as a screen on contrary evidence, is a plausible candidate. The model can explain how rational people, doing the best they can with the evidence they have, can nonetheless form a *group* that is irrational.

THE DANGER TODAY

In her groundbreaking work on the dynamics of public opinion, political scientist Elisabeth Noelle-Neumann argued that certain conditions can create a "spiral of silence," where only one side of an issue is publicly defended. The core mechanism she identifies is this: people don't want to say things that they believe might risk eliciting the disapproval of others; they don't want to potentially lose friends and get pushed out of their social groups. There is a fear of *isolation*. So, instead of saying what they really think about a particular issue, such individuals keep mum. Once the process is set in motion, more and more people become silent about their true opinions.[14]

Spirals like these typically occur with regards to contentious, emotionally laden moral and political issues. A spiral of silence can drive even the majority opinion underground if the minority is sufficiently vocal, and especially if mass media repeatedly and concordantly come down on one side of the issue. Eventually, the spiral of silence causes the majority opinion to effectively disappear, while the previously minority opinion becomes the dominant societal assumption.[15]

What does this mean for us, now? Well for one, we shouldn't assume, for all the reasons explored so far, that such spirals of silence induced by social pressure (real or perceived) are going to line up with the truth all the time (or even most of the time). Spirals of silence are sensitive to *social* forces, not to the *truth*. Thus, they can cause society to settle on opinions that are quite misguided.

However, in order to know what policies to support or how to remedy various social problems, we need to have an accurate idea of what the social world is like. The very best of intentions can have terrible consequences if those intentions are not supplemented with an accurate picture of the world. (Indeed, under some description, more or less all of the worst actors and movements in history can be said to have "good intentions.") But social pressure can warp our collective picture of the world without individuals being in good positions to detect the distortion. So, the more we allow spirals of silence to occur, the more chance there is for the road to hell to be paved with good intentions.

The danger we face today is that many of us have quite confident views about lots of contentious issues, as well as lots of issues that have been "settled," not via a process of institutionalized disconfirmation, but rather through spirals of silence. But this means that the steps we might take to mitigate economic and social problems could backfire, making things worse. The risk becomes greater the more radical, as opposed to piecemeal, solutions we embrace. We might also be misdiagnosing what the problems are in the first place. And we might be missing various forests for the trees. Our Chernobyl, so to speak, might not involve a nuclear powerplant, but might instead manifest itself in the way we conceive of and try to solve social and economic problems.

One way to respond to this predicament is to encourage epistemic humility.[16] Perhaps we should all just check ourselves. This however, is far easier said than done. Knowing our epistemic limitations in abstract terms may not actually induce humility in us (especially the loudest among us) when the rubber meets the road. The only way to properly mitigate our dangerous blind spots is for courageous individuals to speak their minds, and refuse to buckle to social pressure. This is not to say that epistemic humility and other tools for critical thinking are not important or worth cultivating. But if knowledge is a collective enterprise, individual epistemic humility can only go so far. This humility, for instance, cannot prevent a Chernobyl—only people sharing their evidence can.

UPSHOTS FOR CONFORMITY AND COOPERATION

Whenever there is social pressure to support one particular conclusion and to refrain from giving reasons to doubt that conclusion, there will be a systematic filtering out of important information. If, in the end, the group's conclusion is correct, it will be an accident, a stroke of luck. Even then, the group's picture of the world will likely be warped in some way or another. Depending on the context, such distortions can have terrible practical consequences as well.

Two qualifications are in order. First, there is often stigma attached to obviously irrational "giving of evidence." Imagine a person who says "Hey, here's some evidence for thinking the sun goes around the Earth: horses have four legs." People would probably think there's something off with this person, or that he's joking in some way; the argument is a *non sequitur*. Though, people presumably won't get *mad* at him. They'll probably just try to make sure he's not having some kind of breakdown. Second, there are pressures to be relevant in conversation. Thus, giving evidence about the employment effects of minimum wage, say, is not relevant in the context of an ongoing conversation about how the dinosaurs went extinct, and would rightly be frowned upon.

But society often applies pressure on us to conceal evidence in a way that is independent of the quality of the evidence *qua* support for a particular conclusion, or considerations of relevance. Thus, imagine a person giving evidence about the effects of minimum wage, which conflicts with the convictions of her social group, in the context of political discussion. Even if her arguments are good, there will be an inclination for people to act as if to say, "Which side are you on?" or "You're not the good person I thought you were." Or imagine giving reasons to believe in evolution by natural selection within the context of a deeply religious sect of a particular sort. There, people might suspect that the person making such arguments is actually a closet disbeliever, to be shunned.

These forms of social pressure, which come apart from the perceived badness of the argument or evidence on offer, are ubiquitous with regards to ideas that social groups have an affective investment in. The pressures are often tied to issues regarding which taking a particular stand is important to people's identity in some way—be it social, political, religious, national, or professional. What's more, people will often publicly display anger towards those who share evidence supporting disfavored conclusions of this sort.

It is these kinds of pressures, especially when they apply to topics of great epistemic importance or generality—like the theory of evolution or the effects of minimum wage—that can lead to worrisome blind spots. Therefore, providing evidence that challenges prevalent opinion, at personal cost, can be a useful service to society.

Of course, it's important not to overstate the point. A pure contrarian, that is, someone who disagrees with people for the sake of disagreement, is probably not doing much of a service to society. First of all, most people and groups, most of the time, get most things right. If that's correct, then pure contrarians will be wrong most of the time. Secondly, a pure contrarian's opinions will not contain much "signal"—since he disagrees simply because he wants to disagree, people won't be in a good position to take him seriously.

Legal scholar Cass Sunstein, in explaining the perils of conformity thus warns that "We should not lament social influences or wish them away. Much of the time, people do better when they take close account of what others do."[17] Many of the conventions and social norms that societies adopt serve useful functions. Furthermore, even if the contentious issues that generate disagreement or social pressure seem pervasive, they reflect the tip of an iceberg. In almost any society, there is a base of mutual agreement on facts and norms. Most members of most societies agree that theft is wrong, that plants need water to grow, that two and two make four, and that it makes sense to drive on the side of the road on which everybody else is driving. If there was constant disagreement about everything, society, with all the coordination and cooperation it requires, would be impossible.

The tendency to come to mutual agreement with others would have had enormous evolutionary import for our ancestors. Cooperating with others to hunt large game, for example, would have required a lot of agreement and coordination. The hunters would all have to agree about which kind of animal to hunt, what technique to use, what roles each individual must play, how to divide the bounty, and so on. Agreement, then, is indispensable for cooperation, which in turn is indispensable for human society.[18]

Yet, conformity also has a dark side. Individuals who speak their minds despite the pressure serve a crucial function. Sunstein goes on to say, "But social influences also diminish the total level of information within any group, and they threaten, much of the time, to lead individuals and institutions in the wrong directions. Dissent can be an important corrective; many groups and institutions have too little of it . . . conformists are free riders, whereas dissenters often confer benefits on others."[19]

INSTITUTIONS OF KNOWLEDGE PRODUCTION

Social pressure creates blind spots by making it costly to provide evidence on one side of an issue, while making it costless or even beneficial to provide evidence on the other side of the issue. Whenever such incentives exist, we should suspect that our resulting view of the world is warped in some way. These incentives are particularly important to address within the institutions responsible for knowledge production and dissemination: research groups of various sorts and fields and academic departments within the university system.

Given modern division of labor, such institutions specialize in knowledge production; the rest of society thus relies upon them for providing an accurate picture of the world. Other individuals in society, however, do not have the time or resources to check all the work produced by such institutions, and so an element of trust is necessary. Analogously, you don't have the time or wherewithal to check all the work done by your lawyer, doctor, or accountant—when it comes to your interaction with such specialists, then, an element of trust is involved.

However, social pressures within institutions responsible for knowledge production can undermine their mission and distort their product. Science works well only in a context of institutionalized disconfirmation: that is, a situation wherein researchers are free and even incentivized to disconfirm any and all hypotheses that are in contention.

Over time, science has disconfirmed hypotheses that would seem exceedingly natural to humans observing their world. Many things that seem intuitive to us turned out to be false. The Earth, it turned out, is roughly spherical, though it looks flat from our vantage point. And while the sun looks like it goes around the Earth, the reverse is true. In the 17th century, Galileo Galilei suffered persecution at the hands of the Catholic Church for defending this idea. Science naturally works best when such costs are absent—so that it doesn't take a Galilean personality to seek the truth.[20]

Modern physics has upended our intuitive picture of the world even further. The things that look "solid" to us—tables, rocks, books, etc.—are actually made mostly of empty space.[21] And the fundamental units of physical reality have both particle-like and wavelike properties. Albert Einstein famously showed that time is not absolute. Whether or not two spatially distant events are simultaneous depends on the observer's frame of reference. He further showed that space and time are intertwined in such a way that it's best to think of them as spacetime. According to the best models we currently have to explain the behavior of large objects, gravity is the result of spacetime "bending" around massive objects.[22] Trippy stuff!

How has science made these remarkable discoveries that are so far from our intuitive sense of the world? Science is a collaborative effort, and no one person can do it all by themselves, even within a sub-sub-field. Science involves enormous division of labor. But for us to be able to trust the products of science, the incentives have to be right. The incentives that individual scientists face must be aligned with finding the truth, wherever it may lie. Generally, this is the case, and that is why science has been on the whole very successful. In physics or chemistry, if you are able to find experimental data that disconfirms an important and commonly accepted hypothesis, you will receive many professional goods—you'll likely get published in prestigious journals like *Nature* or *Science*, you might get big grants in the future, an endowed chair, maybe even the Nobel Prize.

Given these incentives, physics and chemistry are *self-correcting*. If a hypothesis is easily disconfirmed, it won't last for long. Researchers, incentivized to disconfirm it, will quickly design experiments to show why the hypothesis doesn't hold. Sloman and Fernbach write: "Scientific claims can be checked. If scientists are not telling the truth about a result or if they make a mistake, eventually they are likely to be found out because, if the issue is important enough, someone will try and fail to replicate their result."[23] Many scientists have echoed the importance of this feature of science over the years. Any time the accepted wisdom strays from the truth then, a course-correction will quickly follow.

Understanding knowledge production as a collective endeavor, which relies heavily on a well-maintained epistemic commons, helps us appreciate why John Stuart Mill defended his somewhat radical sounding account of justification for our scientific beliefs in *On Liberty*. He wrote:

> If even the Newtonian philosophy were not permitted to be questioned, mankind could not feel as complete assurance of its truth as they now do. The beliefs which we have most warrant for, have no safeguard to rest on, but a standing invitation to the whole world to prove them unfounded.[24]

Thus, imagine if critics of Newton's physics found themselves unemployable or prone to receiving censure, threats, etc., as soon as they challenged part of the view. Could a person living in Mill's time, circa the mid-19th century, be able to trust the science of physics? Could he have reasonably believed in Newton's laws if people faced a very uphill battle in trying to disconfirm them and he knew about this situation? Plausibly not. For, especially if this person is not a physicist, he lacks the wherewithal to check the researchers' work. For all he knows there may be good reasons to reject Newtonian physics that are just not allowed to surface.

Indeed, as it turns out, Newtonian physics was accurate only in approximation. For macroscopic objects traveling at relatively low speeds, i.e., well below the speed of light, Newton's laws allow us to make approximately true predictions. However, as Einstein later showed, some decades after Mill had passed away, Newtonian physics breaks down when it comes to objects moving close to the speed of light. Furthermore, while Newton assumed that space, time, and mass are absolute, Einstein showed that they are relative. Which events are simultaneous, how long an object is, how much mass it has, all depend on the observer's frame of reference. If you are traveling at, say, half the speed of light relative to where I stand, then the length of a particular table will be quite different for you as opposed to me. Hence, even Newtonian physics, which was by Mill's time well established and confirmed with countless experiments, turned out not to be sacrosanct.

The scientific *process*, then, must be structured in a certain way for it to merit our trust and reliance. If there were contrary evidence to be found, would it be discovered, published, and incorporated into the mainstream scientific consensus? The answer to this question must be yes.

In some sense, the scientific enterprise must be *objective*. What does such objectivity mean? Philosopher Helen Longino argues that it requires an openness to what she calls *transformative critique*. For Longino, science is fundamentally a social practice, and it is precisely due to this fact that its objectivity can be secured. Individual researchers are bound to have their idiosyncratic perspectives and biases. However, "science" is not simply the aggregation of the findings of individual scientists. Science is fundamentally practiced by social groups, not lone individuals. What gets counted as scientific knowledge results from social processes like peer review, attempts at replication, citation patterns, and clashes between defenders of alternative hypotheses and paradigms. This is a feature, not a bug. "Only if the products of inquiry are understood to be formed by the kind of critical discussion that is possible among a plurality of individuals about a commonly accessible phenomenon," says Longino, "can we see how they count as knowledge rather than opinion."[25] Consequently, the more diverse points of view there are within a scientific community, the more objective the process is likely to be.

These lessons are not limited to science. Philosophy or literary criticism can be objective in this way too, according to Longino. However, the objectivity essentially depends on whether the social conditions within the field allow for robust critical discussion. A healthy field of inquiry, one whose product we have reason to take seriously, has to be one where people are incentivized to critique and disagree with ideas, such that no idea is sacred or beyond criticism.

To fix ideas, consider the philosophical field of metaethics. This subdiscipline asks foundational questions about the nature and epistemology of moral claims. These questions include, but are not limited to, the following. Are there any moral facts? If there are moral facts, are they subjective or objective? Would such facts be the sort of thing that can be discovered and investigated by the methods of natural science? How might we come to possess moral knowledge? When we say "murder is wrong," are we expressing something more like a belief or something more like an emotion?[26]

Now metaethics, given my own impression of it, is a good example of a field that is working reasonably well. People defending a wide range of positions—naturalism, non-naturalism, error theory, expressivism, constructivism, Humeanism—have climbed to the top of the profession, winning prestigious awards and endowed chairs, working at elite universities, and so on. A variety of perspectives and styles of argument can thus exist and flourish within the discipline. There's no stigma, as far as I can tell, attached to working on either side of the various debates in metaethics. Consequently, younger members of the profession feel free to follow the argument where it leads. And so, many different kinds of positions within the logical space have renowned and well-respected defenders.[27]

When we look at the product of this discipline then, we can be fairly confident that few stones have been left unturned. If there was an easy argument to be made against some position, it likely will have been made; the remaining fruits on the tree will probably be pretty high up. We don't have to worry about reasons piling up on one side of the debate but being filtered out and discarded on the other side. Part of why metaethics works as well as it does might have to do with the fact that its subject matter—though fascinating and stimulating—does not "excite the passions." People just aren't going to get mad at you for defending non-naturalism or expressivism.

Due to the absence of such social pressure, we find each position having several defenders. This in turn reinforces the willingness of metaethicists to follow the argument where it leads. There's a kind of strength in numbers. Contrast this with a hypothetical scenario where there are 100 naturalists (i.e. those who believe that moral properties are natural properties, in principle investigable by natural science) for every non-naturalist (those who deny naturalism). In such a case, it is hard to imagine not feeling isolation or social pressure against defending non-naturalism. Such pressure, whether real or perceived, would especially impact early career researchers, such as graduate students, whose future careers are uncertain. A promising graduate student who is inclined to defend non-naturalism might think twice. The fact that naturalists are in the overwhelming majority may be taken by such a student—whether consciously or subconsciously, rightly or wrongly—to suggest that defending non-naturalism is a bad career move.

Suppose now we add a stigma to this. Imagine that defenders of non-naturalism were publicly censured and ascribed bad character traits. We can see how this would cause reasons to pile up on one side of the debate. It would create perverse incentives that should undermine the trust we ought to have in the product of this community of research. Fortunately, as it stands, such pressures do not exist within metaethics. In fact, it would be considered grossly unprofessional to publicly ascribe bad character traits to one's intellectual opponents within the field. A person who engaged in ad hominem attacks would quickly lose standing in the profession.

I have been describing modern physics, chemistry, and metaethics as fields that model healthy atmospheres of research (though of course they may not be perfect). But is this true across the board with respect to our institutions of knowledge production? Along with others, economist Glenn Loury suggests there is reason to worry. In a provocative 1994 article called "Self-Censorship in Public Discourse," he writes:

> Some areas of social science inquiry are so closely linked in the public mind to sensitive issues of policy that an objective, scholarly discussion of them is now impossible. Instead of open debate—where participants are prepared to be persuaded by arguments and evidence contrary to their initial presumptions, we have become accustomed to rhetorical contests—where competing camps fire volleys of data and tendentious analyses back and forth at each other.[28]

In a later passage, Loury claims that perverse incentives within a community of research can reduce the degree to which we should take its output seriously:

> The notion of objective research—on the employment effects of the minimum wage, say, or the influence of maternal employment on child development—can have no meaning if, when the results are reported, other 'scientists' are mainly concerned to pose the ad hominem query: 'Just what kind of economist, sociologist, and so on would say this?' Not only will investigators be induced to censor themselves, the very way in which research is evaluated and in which consensus about 'the facts' is formed will be altered. If when a study yields unpopular conclusions it is subjected to greater scrutiny, and more effort is expended toward its refutation, an obvious bias to 'find what the community is looking for' will have been introduced. Thus the very way in which knowledge of the world around us is constituted can be influenced by the phenomenon of strategic expression.[29]

To the extent Loury is right, our epistemic condition with respect to the output of fields that are politicized in the way he describes above is shaky. Given the mountains and mountains of evidence relevant to all these policy-adjacent debates, though, none of us has the time, energy, or expertise required to dig through everything and properly make up our own minds. We inevitably have to rely on the journals, textbooks, and public lectures of the practitioners of these fields. But if the incentives within these fields are skewed in the way Loury describes, then such reliance will expose us to a lopsided selection and analysis of the facts out there. Depending on the case, this may well put us in a *worse* position epistemically than either ignorance or suspension of judgment with respect to certain topics. It would be like a jury being made to hear hours of arguments from the prosecution, and zero from the defense. Likely, the jury would have been better off before, when they had no opinion on the case!

All this puts us in a serious predicament, *especially* because, unlike metaethics (sorry metaethicists), the kinds of research Loury alludes to are extremely important to get right from a practical, policy-making perspective. The proper maintenance of the epistemic commons, when it comes to such fields of knowledge, then, is all the more important.

CONCLUSION

Social pressure to conceal evidence can create blind spots that can often be dangerous. Any time there is social pressure of this kind, we should suspect that our view of the world is distorted in important ways. What's the ethical upshot of this? If this is right, what should we, *as individuals*, do? That is the topic of the next chapter.

Two

Let us not concur casually about the most important matters.
—Heraclitus (DK 47)

CONFORMISM AS FREE RIDING

Free riding is tempting. But we typically think it's unethical. At the very least, we don't see free riders as exemplars of moral virtue. Think of the roommate who shirks on the cleaning tasks because he knows the others will do them. Or think of the person who never picks up after their dog when walking through a park. Or imagine a person who drives a gas guzzling Hummer and never recycles. All these characters rely on others to do important work which they themselves benefit from—keeping the house clean, the park sanitary, the environment non-degraded—but aren't willing to put in the required effort themselves.

In general, whenever something is a common resource, people are tempted to free ride in this way. A clean sink, park, or atmosphere are common resources in the sense that it's not possible or feasible to exclude people from deriving the associated benefits. A clean atmosphere benefits everybody. Yet, for each person, the costs involved in keeping it clean—i.e. recycling, driving more efficient cars, eating less meat, etc.—outweigh the benefits accrued to *that* person by *her* actions to keep it clean. So, it's nice to have a clean park, but perhaps for many, the effort involved in picking up after their dog is not worth the extra cleanliness that results from the vantage point of the individual. In other words, the costs are concentrated but the benefits are distributed. Any situation with this structure generates the temptation to free ride.

I have been arguing that there is an *epistemic* commons in an important sense as well. Our epistemic health depends on the epistemic health of others, due to the division of cognitive labor. For one, we can't verify everything ourselves. Furthermore, our patterns of thinking are deeply influenced by those in our surrounding culture. Pressures to suppress evidence can lead to avoidable and potentially dangerous distortions of our view of the world. In cases like the dam described in the previous chapter, or the Chernobyl nuclear plant accident, such distortions have far reaching, disastrous consequences. Just as it is important to preserve the health of the physical commons—our atmosphere, rivers, oceans, etc.—it is important to preserve the health of our epistemic commons, viz., the stock of evidence and perspectives alive within the communities we're part of.

The problem is a commons problem because typically everyone benefits (at least in the long run) from their community having a better picture of the world. Everyone involved with the dam case of the previous chapter is better off if information is freely shared. Likewise, presumably all parties would have been better off if the evidential bottlenecks leading to the Chernobyl disaster had been avoided. These cases involve practical considerations—the disaster has an enormous practical impact (uniformly negative) on all parties. But we can make the same point in purely epistemic terms as well. The group of partisans described above is such that all individuals would benefit epistemically—i.e. their own picture of the world would become more accurate—if information were freely shared among members.

The issue, however, is that the perceived costs are concentrated. If Alice, in the partisan group described in the previous chapter, shares her evidence about crime and policing with others, then, as far as she can tell, she will lose standing within the group, but the (epistemic) benefits of her contribution will be spread out. Analogously, the lazy roommate's efforts to clean the dishes involve a concentrated cost to him but the benefits of a clean sink are enjoyed by everyone in the house. Thus, in both cases, there is a temptation to free ride.

In both these cases, it is *rational* in one sense to free ride. Assuming that the other roommates let him get away with it, the lazy roommate maximizes self-interest, construed narrowly, by allowing others to clean while he relaxes. Similarly, the person who doesn't pick up after their dog enjoys the benefits of a clean park while shirking the cost. Likewise, I want to add, conformists obtain benefits from a well-maintained epistemic commons while allowing others, i.e. dissenters, to do the hard work. This may not be irrational from the vantage point of self-interest, construed narrowly.

Now, I am not alone in making this observation. Sunstein emphasizes this aspect of conformity in the quote presented in the last chapter. Dan Kahan and colleagues, known for their work on cultural cognition and motivated reasoning, echo the idea:

> It is perfectly rational, *from an individual-welfare perspective*, for individuals to engage decision-relevant science in a manner that promotes culturally or politically congenial

beliefs. What any individual member of the public thinks about the reality of climate change, the hazards of nuclear waste disposal, or the efficacy of gun control is too inconsequential to influence the risk that that person or anyone he or she cares about faces. Nevertheless, given what positions on these issues signify about a person's defining commitments, forming a belief at odds with the one that predominates on it within important affinity groups of which such a person is a member could expose him or her to an array of highly unpleasant consequences.[1]

Others have pointed out that being an informed voter is in fact *irrational*, unless you simply enjoy being informed or think there are strong enough moral reasons to be informed. The idea is this. Being an informed voter takes a lot of time and effort. It involves looking closely at complicated bills and voting records. It also involves learning a lot of economics, reflecting carefully on public policy, being aware of various data, and so on. So, all this goes on the cost side of the ledger. What goes on the benefit side? Well, you might cast an informed vote. But individual votes almost never make a difference. The chance of your flipping a national or even statewide election is exceedingly small. So, there's not much accruing on the benefit side at all. Hence, most voters are *rationally* ignorant about the important issues.[2]

However, what I want to emphasize here is that we're often not in a position to know *how* the evidence we have will contribute to the epistemic health of the group. Our evidence may well be a crucial part of either eliminating the blind spot or changing the incentives of others so that they will reveal evidence that cures the collective blind spot. And this might be worth the cost for us given what we care about, or what we should care about. While the notion of speaking your mind can be interpreted in different ways, this chapter will focus on the moral dimensions of individuals sharing their evidence.

DAM AND ENGINEERS REDUX

Consider again the case of the engineers and the dam, from the previous chapter. Suppose one of the engineers, the one with the evidence denoted by 'R_3,' comes forward and shares her information. Now, R_3 becomes common knowledge. Well, it then becomes clear to the other two engineers that they should come forward with their information—for now, their sharing information becomes manifestly consequential.

As I set up the case, each piece of counterevidence—i.e. evidence supporting the conclusion that the dam will break— is not enough, by itself, to defeat R_1 and R_2. It is only when you take R_3, R_4, and R_5 together that you can conclude that the dam is going to break, despite R_1 and R_2. Now, evidence functions in a myriad of different ways. But to make things simple, let's suppose that the evidence here works in a linear and aggregative fashion. Each piece of evidence, let's suppose, has a weight of one. And the evidence adds up as weights do on a scale. So, if R_1 and R_2 are on one side of the scale, and if only *one* of the other pieces of evidence is on the other side, then the scale tips in favor of thinking the dam will not break. If R_3, R_4, and R_5 are together on the other side, however, then the scale tips in favor of thinking the dam will break. As things stand, each engineer knows only one of the con reasons, and so from each engineer's vantage point the dam is safe, and there's no point in coming forward with worrisome evidence, only to invite social opprobrium. But the crucial thing is that no engineer knows that the others are in possession of evidence such that *were* it to be revealed, the thing to conclude would be that the dam is going to break.

But when one of the engineers comes forward with R_3, the reasons come into equipoise from the vantage point of either of the other engineers. Consider what their weight scales will look like. One of the remaining engineers will know R_1 and R_2, on the pro side, and R_3 and R_4, on the con side. The other engineer will know R_1 and R_2, on the pro side, and R_3 and R_5, on the con side. So, from both their vantage points, the dam may well really break but they can't be sure—the weight scale is in balance, so to speak.

But now, the reasoning that says "my evidence won't make a difference anyway" does not work. Each of the remaining engineers now has evidence that they definitively *should* reveal, even from a narrowly self-interested perspective. If it's up in the air whether the dam will break, given the evidence, then serious discussion and further testing should follow. This would thus incentivize the other engineers to reveal their evidence and seek discussion about the real possibility of breakage.

So then suppose one of the others comes forward, with R_4. Well, it is now clear to the last holdout that the dam is going to break—for now, he has all the relevant evidence: R_1 through R_5. Since the breaking of the dam is terrible from the perspective of what he cares about, we can assume, he will share the last piece of evidence if he's minimally rational. Catastrophe will thus be avoided.

What I want to show with the use of this example is that we're often not in a position to tell how our evidence impacts the overall case for a particular claim, and, moreover, how it might change the incentives of *others* with respect to revealing their own evidence. The key point is that the presence of social pressure can obscure the evidential landscape for the groups we're part of. Thus, whenever there is social pressure to avoid revealing evidence, we should *suspect*—though we can't tell for sure—that an important blind spot exists. We may not know how exactly our evidence might bear upon epistemic commons. We don't know whether it will be the crucial piece that clears away a misunderstanding or shows some matter in an important new light. It may well be inconsequential, but then again, it may not. When social pressure obscures the evidential landscape, then, the problem becomes deeper than the one described by Kahan and colleagues.

A DUTY TO SPEAK YOUR MIND

Whenever there is social pressure to refrain from revealing some evidence we have, I contend, we should take ourselves to have a duty to reveal that evidence—it is in this sense that we have a duty to speak our minds. It is a *prima facie* duty: i.e., one that need not be decisive in all contexts. For example, we have a *prima facie* duty not to break promises. But if breaking a promise to get lunch with a friend is the only way you can save someone's life, then you should obviously break the promise.[3]

Indeed, sometimes the costs of revealing forbidden evidence will be prohibitive. Imagine a person eking out survival within Stalin's Soviet Union. Stalin conducted regular purges and orchestrated the killings of hundreds of thousands who showed the slightest signs of dissent. In many 20th century communist regimes, people could face execution for expressing evidence to the effect that particular policies were not working as intended or that the rations were too small for their families.[4] In such gruesome contexts, it is too much to expect people to speak their minds—morality cannot be *that* demanding.

However, in many situations, the costs, though they exist, are nowhere near facing execution or death-by-labor in a Soviet gulag. The costs for us, living in modern democracies, can often be real. In the worst case, they might involve losing your job and having to find other employment. But often, the costs might just involve small losses in social or professional status. The partisans in the example mentioned earlier likely won't get fired for revealing dissenting information about crime or abortion. They may well, however, lose some standing amongst their social group. Nonetheless, this cost is not prohibitive. Morality cannot be too demanding, but it does make demands on us—it instructs us in many cases to forgo narrow self-interest for wider goods.

If morality never instructed us to sacrifice narrow self-interest, then no case of free riding would be objectionable (besides a whole host of other bad behavior). It would then not be wrong to litter, pollute heavily, let others do the dishes, and so on. But surely such behaviors are wrong because they rely on the cooperation of others while offering no cooperation from one's own end. Whenever social pressure exists to suppress one's evidence, then, I claim there is a prima facie duty to defy that pressure—i.e. share one's evidence despite the social costs, so long as those costs are not prohibitively high.

This is just a natural extension of the way we think of our ordinary moral obligations in a variety of commons contexts: we have a prima facie duty not to free ride, unless doing so would be prohibitive. Hence, we can understand a poor fisherman who overfishes a lake to feed his family. The costs of cooperation for him—namely, not being able to feed his family—are too high. But we rightly frown upon a healthy, able individual who does not pick up after their dog, or a person who doesn't recycle even if the option is available and easily accessible to them.

IMPERFECT DUTIES AND KEEPING YOUR POWDER DRY

What exactly does the duty to speak your mind amount to? In other words, if there is such a duty, when does it recommend us to share our evidence? A natural model suggested by the discussion so far is the following:

> *Whenever* there is a social pressure not to share piece of evidence E, and the cost of doing so for you does not meet some threshold T, you should share E.

As described earlier, the presence of social pressure not to reveal certain evidence suggests the likely presence of a blind spot. Revealing one's evidence may then be an important corrective and a service to others vis-à-vis the proper maintenance of the epistemic commons. On the other hand, it is not plausible that morality is so demanding that it requires individuals to share their evidence even in the face of execution or imprisonment. The principle above would thus seem to capture both these desiderata.

However, the principle as stated faces several problems. The first is the grandma's ugly sweater problem. Suppose your grandmother knits a sweater for you as a gift for Christmas. It turns out that you don't like the design, and it's not really your style. Should you say this as you tear off the wrapping paper? Obviously not. But this case would seem to meet the conditions outlined in the principle above. There is social pressure to avoid saying you don't like it: your family will likely frown on you for saying this. And the costs are not prohibitive—you're not getting sent to the gulag. What's going on in this case? Well, one key feature here is that the underlying matter is not of broad importance. In contrast, the cases we looked at earlier did involve matters of broad social importance—the stability of a dam, the proper policy with respect to crime, the ethics of abortion, and the like. Thus, plausibly, the duty to share evidence would seem to kick in only when the matter at hand is of sufficient importance.

The second problem is that even if the principle may not be too demanding in any one particular case, following the principle *all the time* would make morality too demanding. Consider: it is not too demanding for me to give $100 to a well-run charity. But if there are one hundred such charities, the requirement to donate $100 to *each* well-run charity would make morality too demanding given my financial situation and family responsibilities. Likewise, it may be too demanding to require of people that they share evidence in every single case where there is social pressure not to, even in cases where the matter at hand is of sufficient importance.

What this suggests is that we should understand the duty to share our evidence as an *imperfect* duty. Immanuel Kant famously made the distinction between perfect and imperfect duties.[5] The former yield determinate prescriptions, and don't allow for any discretion or latitude. For instance, you should not steal your neighbor's car so as to sell it and go on a nice vacation. It's just not to be done, period. Kant also thought we have duties of beneficence to others and duties to ourselves for self-improvement. But a duty of beneficence does not yield a determinate prescription. It can be discharged in many ways: by volunteering at a local cleanup effort, by being a helping friend, and so on. A duty of self-improvement can also be discharged in many ways. For example, if such a duty involves getting in better physical shape, then you can do so by taking up running, cycling, swimming, or weight training. There's a lot of room for latitude and discretion.

In a similar vein, philosopher Jennifer Lackey develops a characterization of a duty to object (roughly, a duty to correct falsehoods) in terms of an imperfect duty. She writes:

> Just as I ought to generally contribute to the moral flourishing of others so, too, should I do my part in ensuring that false and unjustified beliefs aren't promulgated. But surely I need not step in every time. If there were no discretion allowed, I would quite literally need to spend all of the hours in the day objecting to what is said on the news, in my Facebook feed, at the dinner table, and so on.[6]

Like the duty of beneficence then, the duty to object, for Lackey, is an imperfect one. Lackey contends that how much we are required to do in order to fulfill such a duty depends on two further things: (i) our social standing and (ii) what the others in our group are already doing. The greater our social standing (status, wealth, etc.) the more we are required to do. For one, people with higher social standing will have more of an impact with their speech. Further, they will often have lower costs—a tenured professor risks less than a graduate student, for example. Regarding (ii), if others are already doing a lot to object, in Lackey's sense, then a smaller burden falls on our shoulders. Thus, we're required to do less if others are doing their fair share. Compare: if lots of other people are giving to charity, there's a lesser need for us to give as much. But if relatively few people are giving, then the duty of beneficence will demand more from us in terms of charitable donation.

The duty to share evidence in the face of social pressure will have similar structural features. Sharing one's evidence in the face of every single instance of social pressure not to do so (even in cases which do not run afoul of the grandma's sweater problem) would be too demanding. Note also that since the duty I am positing is a duty to share one's evidence in the face of social pressure, so long as the costs are not too great, it accommodates Lackey's qualifications automatically. If lots of other people are sharing a particular piece of evidence, then almost ipso facto the social pressure against doing so will be small. But costless sharing of evidence is not what the duty amounts to. I have no duty to say that the Earth revolves around the sun now: there's no cost for me in doing so. But one might have that duty circa the late 17th century. Second, since costs matter, tenured professors, for example, will often have more of a duty to share certain pieces of evidence than graduate students who might risk unemployment by doing so.

Finally, a third problem the proposal outlined above faces is that it's often wise to keep the powder dry. The phrase originates from the 17th century when English general and statesman Oliver Cromwell advised his soldiers to keep their gunpowder dry. If you got your gunpowder wet back then, you couldn't fire when needed—and so it was important strategically to mind your resources and be well prepared. Analogously, if you never take heed of social pressure and go against the grain all the time, you might develop a reputation as a contrarian even if you are not. Such a reputation can "poison the well," and cause people not to take you seriously. Depending on the context, for example, such behavior might signal to others that you are part of the outgroup. And empirical evidence suggests that people are prone to quickly discount the testimony of outgroup members. Sunstein explains: "If people seem to be from some group we distrust or dislike, or a kind of 'out group,' they are far less likely to influence us, even on the simplest questions. Indeed, we might say or do the very opposite ('reactive devaluation')."[7]

Thus, one must be somewhat forward-looking in order to fulfill one's duty to properly maintain the epistemic commons. The latitude and discretion characteristic of Kantian imperfect duties include a *strategic* element here as well. Of course, what strategy is appropriate will be heavily context dependent, in a way that makes any general recommendations otiose.

SHARING EVIDENCE VS CONTRARIANISM AND TROLLING

If Sunstein is right, then conformists are free riders: hence, their behavior leaves something to be desired, morally speaking. But on the other end, a pure contrarian cannot be a paragon of virtue either. Recall that the pure contrarian disagrees with others simply for the sake of disagreement. Perhaps he gets a kick out of disagreeing with others, and thus disagrees merely for that reason. Such characters are, obviously, rare. Most people want to fit in with others. But nonetheless, the contrarian is a possibility we should keep in mind. The virtuous person in this regard, it would seem, lies in the mean of the two extremes—conformism on the one end and contrarianism on the other.

There is another related but perhaps more mischievous character: the troll. The troll is someone who enjoys getting people riled up. Trolls are common particularly within anonymous online discourse, and if they're defending fashionable opinions, even non-anonymous online discourse. A troll will say something he knows will provoke a strong emotional reaction from others—in particular anger, frustration, or disillusionment. Moreover, he says what he does *in order to* provoke that reaction. His goal is thus not to arrive at the truth on some matter or improve the discourse in some way.

It would be bad if the duty I have been positing so far entailed that such characters are doing something good. Fortunately, it does not. The duty is a duty to share one's *evidence* in the face of contrary social pressure. What is evidence? Philosopher Thomas Kelly explains: "Intuitively, one's evidence is *what one has to go on* in arriving at a view. Evidence is what Sherlock Holmes carefully collects and surveys, and that from which he ultimately infers the identity of the person who committed the crime."[8] Rational thinkers arrive at their beliefs by properly basing them on the total evidence they have. This means that evidence can come in many shapes and sizes—it might involve direct perception, arguments, datasets and statistical analyses, or the testimony of others, among other things. These can all be proper bases for forming particular beliefs.

To fix ideas, suppose the issue at hand is crime and policing. For example, we might be interested in whether increased police presence within an area reduces violent crime. What's the relevant evidence here? Well it might include things like crime statistics in various neighborhoods along with data about police presence. It may also include first-hand accounts of individuals in various neighborhoods.

Now suppose there is social pressure within your reference network against giving evidence for a particular view about policing and crime. It is here that the *prima facie* imperfect duty to share evidence kicks in. Importantly, the evidence has to be actual evidence. Contrast this with what a troll might do: he might anonymously assert an opinion that has no connection to his evidence. He may not have looked at any of the statistics or first-hand accounts; he'll simply say whatever he knows will rile others up. Similarly, a contrarian may just engage in fanciful hypotheticals without having any evidence to back them up. But crucially, these characters are not sharing their *evidence*—namely, whatever it is that would bear upon whether a view about crime and policing is justified. And that's what the duty described in this chapter recommends.

GOOD FAITH

We can share genuine evidence in order to mislead others. Hence, imagine that a detective finds out three pieces of evidence during her investigation. A particular suspect, Jones, was seen entering the house around the time the murder took place. This is a reason to think that Jones is guilty. However, it was Smith's DNA that was found on the crime scene and murder weapon. In addition, Smith has no alibi, while Jones does. So, the overall evidence suggests Smith is guilty, not Jones. But suppose our nefarious detective harbors a grudge against Jones and so wants him to be found guilty. She thus reveals only the first piece of evidence.

This sort of evidence sharing is, paradigmatically, not done in good faith. The detective in this case intentionally makes the epistemic position of the prosecutor and jury *worse*—they were better off before, when they would have suspended judgment about who the culprit was. Now, they have been exposed to evidence, but evidence carefully curated so as to mislead. Plausibly, our duty to share evidence in the face of contrary social pressure cannot be one to share evidence so as to deliberately mislead. Rather, we must do so in *good faith*—where the intention is to improve rather than to further deteriorate the epistemic situations of others.[9]

THE IMPERFECT DUTY GENERALIZED

The duty to share evidence in face of social pressure against doing so is a special case of the more general imperfect duty to improve the condition of our epistemic commons. In analogous fashion, the duty to give to charity (assuming the possession of means do so) is a special case of the more general duty of benevolence. Hence, someone with little by way of pecuniary means can nonetheless fulfill their duty of benevolence in other ways. They may not give money to charity but may nonetheless help others by being a supportive friend or family member, for instance. These aren't mutually exclusive, of course. An excellent way of fulfilling the duty of beneficence for someone who is well off might include donating to charity in addition to being a helping friend or family member.

Similarly, some of us may not be in a position to offer evidence against social pressure. Thus, someone might not have looked too deeply into issues like the minimum wage or crime and policing or abortion. Indeed, this will be true for many of us. We have other things to do with our time: work a nine-to-five job, raise children, exercise, mow the lawn, chat with friends, and much else. However, even in this case, we can do our part in helping to improve the epistemic commons: namely, by doing what we can to alleviate social pressures and taboos against sharing certain types of evidence or perspective.

There are a variety of ways to do this. For example, an academic might stand up for a colleague who is under fire for

Why It's OK to Speak Your Mind

publishing research that is deemed controversial. As I will discuss in detail later, even one voice of support can often make a huge social and psychological impact on others. Typically, this will involve some cost. There will be a good chance that some might treat such a person as being on the wrong "side"—and thus to be shunned and ostracized. And so, standing up for a colleague in this way might well have adverse social and professional repercussions. But of course, as emphasized earlier, morality often instructs us to sacrifice our narrow self-interest, so long as the costs are not excessively high.

Further, those who work in professions responsible for knowledge production and dissemination—academics, journalists, etc.—might take steps to promote intellectual diversity within their professions: for example, by hiring researchers or writers who can offer evidence that might mitigate blind spots. Recent empirical work suggests that there are benefits to both ideological and cognitive diversity when it comes to the output of teams. Teams composed of ideologically/cognitively diverse individuals produce better output (as measured by objective metrics) than ideologically/cognitively homogenous groups.[10]

In general, we might try to defend and uphold social norms in which people can share evidence in a relatively free atmosphere. This is not to say there shouldn't be robust disagreement. You might offer some evidence against claim X while I offer evidence for X. But the key is to promote social norms and structures wherein disagreement doesn't lead to ostracism or shunning.

This is particularly important when those who might share certain types of evidence are in a minority within a given reference network or milieu. Here, the majority have an enormous upper hand and a lot of leeway to intimidate the minority. Thus, suppose that within a particular context, the claim X is held by the majority. Moreover, imagine the majority has some affective investment in believing X. So, it's not simply a "dry" matter to them—like some abstract theorem or obscure polymer. Rather, the matter is close in some way to their social identity.

Such a scenario can likely lead to an atmosphere which can easily prevent the countervailing evidence from surfacing. The majority now will be able to intimidate the minority in a variety of ways. For example, when someone from the majority levels an ad hominem attack against a member of the minority, he might receive little if any pushback. The majority, by stipulation, doesn't want to believe the contrary proposition. Of course, the members of the majority may not explicitly think "I don't want countervailing evidence to surface because it will undermine my justification for this belief that I am psychologically attached to." The inner machinations of our minds are rarely transparent to us. Rather, the temptation will be to see the dissenter as evil or the evidence as fabricated, even when these things are not true. The opportunities, however, for being able to level ad hominem attacks will not be symmetric. If a member of the minority does this, she will be quickly called out by the majority—and rightly so. Ad hominem attacks are not how virtuous and mature people conduct inquiry. But the problem is that the ability to conduct unjustified "warfare" in this way will be profoundly asymmetric.

Another method of intimidation might involve the spread of unjustified rumors. These rumors will spread easily within the community because of what the majority wants to believe. If the dissenters are bad people, there's no reason to take them seriously. On the other hand, unjustified rumors will have a much harder time getting traction in the other direction.

Asymmetric intimidation can also result from uncharitable interpretations and "strawmanning." The majority will be in a position to strawman the dissenters' views, that is, present them as much less reasonable and well-argued-for than they really are. Any attempt by the minority to strawman the majority position, however, will be quickly (and rightly) met with opposition. The same goes for things like public censure, the imposition of professional costs, and so on. While the majority will be able to publicly censure or impose professional costs on the minority, the reverse will not hold.

Here, I am just highlighting a few of the ways in which the ability to impose costs will be asymmetric when there is an ideological majority within a social or professional context. Many of these things work on subtle and subconscious levels—on which, more later. The point of importance here is that one way in which individuals can take steps to improve the epistemic commons, even if they belong to the majority, is to try to curb the majority's tendencies towards such behavior. Thus, for example, someone might resist the temptation to use ad hominem attacks, and further, discourage others from employing such attacks, even if they're friendly to his "side" of the issue. Often, the urge is to do the exact opposite—to *praise* or *applaud* ad hominem attacks when they align with the majority opinion. The rewards are feelings of righteous indignation (if one shares the majority opinion) as well as social status and approval. But again, morality often requires us to forgo such rewards.

In a passage worth quoting at length, John Stuart Mill emphasized similar worries about our behavioral tendencies when it comes to lopsided opinion, regarding which there is widespread affective investment:

The worst offence of this kind which can be committed by a polemic, is to stigmatise those who hold the contrary opinion as bad and immoral men. To calumny of this sort, those who hold any unpopular opinion are peculiarly exposed, because they are in general few and uninfluential, and nobody but themselves feel much interest in seeing justice done them; but this weapon is, from the nature of the case, denied to those who attack a prevailing opinion: they can neither use it with safety to themselves, nor, if they could, would it do anything but recoil on their own cause. In general, opinions contrary to those commonly received can only obtain a hearing by studied moderation of language.[11]

One way to help the epistemic commons, then, is to promote the "studied moderation of language," in Mill's words, as a social norm, regardless of one's actual position vis-à-vis the issue at hand.

I want to emphasize here that "majority opinion," as it relates to social pressures, is not to be construed as relative to an entire country or the whole world. What ultimately matters for people's behavior in this regard is their *reference network*. Something might be a minority opinion with respect to the country's or world's population but a majority (even overwhelming majority) position within a particular industry or social class or professional network. In fact, it can often take enormous courage to defend a view that has widespread acceptance in the general public, depending on one's social and professional context.

The social costs for expressing opinions are heavily context dependent. What might take courage to say in a rural town may not take courage to say in a newsroom, and vice versa.

Within several religious communities across the world, it takes enormous courage to say that atheists should not be punished by law. But it takes no courage at all to say this within a typical university in the U.S.—it would be like saying the sky is blue or that grass is green.

Who counts as a dissenter and who counts as a conformist thus depends on the social context. Recall that this distinction is important if we think of conformism as free riding, in the way discussed earlier. If someone thinks and says the same things as everyone else in his reference network, he's not a dissenter even if his position is a minority position when it comes to the world at large. Rather, he's a conformist. For it's not the world at large that is able to impose social and other costs on him—instead, it is his reference network.

EXPRESSING OPINIONS AND COURAGE

Sometimes, the ad hominem attacker on the side of majority opinion may even be lauded as courageous! But of course, an action that is lauded as courageous and one that is courageous can come apart—particularly where the courage in question is expressive as opposed to physical courage. Can a person who is widely lauded within his social circles for sharing an opinion be courageous in sharing that opinion?

He may be tempted to think so. What psychologists call moral self-enhancement is people's tendency to have a high moral opinion of themselves, especially in comparison to others. In particular, people often attribute to themselves high levels of moral virtues such as honesty and loyalty. There is a well-studied, high degree of irrationality involved here. Paradoxically, the average person judges themselves to be more morally virtuous (on a variety of dimensions) than average.[12]

Naturally, then, people will tend to think of themselves as courageous even as their expressions of opinion are lauded by their milieu.

But what is courage? The ancient Greek thinkers often framed the virtue of courage within the context of war. Aristotle famously analyzed the virtue of courage (or bravery) as he did all virtues: as a mean between two extremes. A cowardly soldier would be excessively afraid to be killed in war. A rash soldier would be excessively fearless, perhaps flying into battle when it's wise to wait. Such a person would be very rare, and "some sort of madman."[13] A courageous soldier would be a proper mean between these two. He would be afraid of the right things at the right time—and he wouldn't be afraid per se of a noble death (according to Aristotle) in war.

But notice we can't apply the concept of courage in this way to a situation that presents no danger at all. One may well be courageous as a person and face a situation with no danger. A courageous soldier might be relaxing under a tree, in a meadow, during a time of total peace. But such a situation will not allow for the *manifestation* of the virtue of courage.[14]

Similarly, then, sharing an opinion that is widely lauded as courageous within one's relevant reference network paradoxically *cannot* involve courage—unless there is a penalty enforced from outside the reference network. For, being widely lauded as courageous is obviously an enormous social benefit. And what is the cost? In war, it may be death. But when it comes to expressing opinions in modern democracies, the costs to be borne are social—yet by stipulation, the person in question is being lauded, and hence receiving *benefits*. This of course, is not true in a case where most of one's reference network lauds us for saying X but doing so publicly might land the person in jail. Imagine, for example, a reference network of early

20th century independence activists working to overthrow a colonial power. Expressing dissent against the colonial power will elicit praise from the reference network, but doing so publicly will risk punishment from the colonial administrators. However, this is typically not the situation we find ourselves in within modern democracies.

Manifesting courage as it relates to sharing our evidence, then, by its nature implies taking risks of being frowned upon, or worse, ostracized, by one's social network. Yet of course, courage can't be had cheaply. It is the very essence of the virtue of courage that it doesn't come painlessly. As Aristotle says, "standing firm against what is painful makes us call people brave; that is why bravery is both painful and justly praised."[15] Now, courage may well be praised by one's reference network when it comes to war—the enemy there is external to that network. But the "pain" or cost involved in sharing our evidence, within the context of modern democracy, is typically imposed by the network itself. So we can't be widely lauded by our social network as courageous while at the same time actually displaying courage. Can't have your cake and eat it too.

MARGINAL VALUE AND HETERODOX RESEARCH

Economists and decision theorists model rational decisions as being made at the *margins*.[16] When consumers buy goods, they base their decisions on the marginal cost and the marginal benefit of the nth unit. Consider, for example, the purchase of cups of coffee. The first might give you more benefit as compared to the cost (let's say it's $3). The second might still benefit you more than $3. But the benefit of the third may be below $3—or, the alternate use to which you could put that $3.

You've already had two cups and gotten a good dose of caffeine. You might have some decaf if it was being sold for 50¢, but at its current price, it's just not worth it.

In this way, the marginal benefit of a typical good decreases for us, while the cost remains the same. The coffee is going to cost $3 regardless of how many you buy (typically) but the benefits of the third cup of coffee are far less than the benefits of the first cup. You stop buying the good when the marginal cost exceeds the marginal benefit—in this hypothetical case, you stop at two cups. The decision, if made rationally, is made at the margins. The question is not "how much are three cups of coffee worth to me, rather than zero?" Three cups of coffee may well be worth $25 to you if the alternative is zero cups. You've just got to have that daily caffeine fix, let's say. But this doesn't mean that you will buy three cups since they cost $9, and 25 is bigger than 9. Rather, in making the decision as to whether to buy the third cup of coffee, you ask yourself "how much is the third cup worth to me?" And here, the answer may well be: less than the $3 that it costs.

Similarly, the third bag of oranges is way less valuable to an individual consumer than the first. Same goes for the third car, the third computer, the third house, the third TV, etc. Of course, there's nothing special about the number three—rather the point is that typically, the value of the marginal unit of a good decreases as the amount of that good we have increases. Thus, the tenth TV is even less valuable than the third for us. Unless one is a filthy rich person with a mansion, she typically won't buy ten TVs or ten cars.

Marginal analysis applies to scenarios beyond just individual purchasing decisions. If you're studying for an exam, the first hour of reviewing the material is much more valuable than the 13th. It might be wise overall to spend that first hour studying rather than hanging out with friends, but by the time you've already studied for 12 hours, it could be a much better use of time to relax and talk to people. Likewise, the first half hour of exercise per day is much more valuable than the next half hour.

The same sort of analysis applies to decisions involving what economists call *public goods*. Public goods are goods that are non-excludable and non-rivalrous. Clean air is a paradigm public good. We can't exclude others from enjoying clean air. And clean air is non-rivalrous in the sense that my enjoying the clean air doesn't affect your ability to enjoy the clean air. Contrast this with a cup of coffee, which is a classic case of a private good. There, you can exclude me from drinking from your cup. And, my drinking your coffee means there's less remaining for you—so it's rivalrous.[17]

The notorious problem with public goods is that they throw our incentives way out of whack. Consider roads. A road is a public good (unless it's a toll road). Everybody benefits from having roads. However, nobody has an incentive to pay for them voluntarily. Let's say that for the road to be built, each person in the town has to contribute $100. Now, the road may be worth way more than $100 to each individual. But this is not the relevant question. The relevant question each individual will consider is: "how much benefit will I receive from contributing $100 to the road project?" Here, the answer will be: very little. To see this, note that adding that money to the project might make the road a quarter of an inch wider. But it's not worth it to you to spend $100 to make one road in your town a quarter inch wider. You might rather put that money towards a comfy chair or a nice dinner—those things would add more to your life-satisfaction. The problem is that everyone will think this way, and so nobody will contribute to the road fund.

But the issue is that *everyone* would be better off if they all contributed to the road fund. After all, the road is worth more than $100 to each of them, as stipulated. Thus, there are gains to be made, from everyone's perspective, left on the table. Enter: the government. The government can make use of coercion to create public goods like roads. It coerces by means of taxation. People don't have a choice as to whether to pay taxes—they can't thus voluntarily decide not to contribute the $100. But, paradoxically, by making the choice to pay taxes involuntary, the government makes them better off.

The provision of public goods in this way has been considered to be one of the main justifications for government. Adam Smith thought the three jobs of government were: (i) provision of national defense; (ii) provision of a justice system; and (iii) "erecting and maintaining those public institutions and those public works, which though they may be in the highest degree advantageous to a great society, are, however, of such a nature, that the profit could never repay the expense to any individual, or small number of individuals; and which it, therefore, cannot be expected that any individual, or small number of individuals, should erect or maintain."[18] Notice that all these functions can be subsumed under the idea of public good provision.

However, the presence of the government as a tool for public good creation doesn't make all the problems associated with public goods go away. Should the next road be built? Rational decision making from the standpoint of the community would consider the total cost of the road and compare it with the benefit the whole community reaps from having the road built. The thing to do then is to keep building until the former quantity is greater than the latter.

But the issue is that communities don't decide to build particular roads. Administrators within the government do. And the rational thing to do for an administrator may come apart from doing what is best for the community. This can cause the under-provision of some public goods, and the over-provision of others. Ideally, of course, a government administrator would only take actions that are to the benefit of the community. But people are not ideal—sometimes they favor themselves or their friends at the expense of the average community member. Within democracies, voters have some control over their administrators, but such control is not perfect—it goes via the channel of representative government, rather than direct democracy on every particular decision to be made. Such is the *principal-agent* problem in government administration.[19]

Now, academic research is a public good—non-excludable and non-rivalrous—and thus presents people with similar kinds of incentives as roads. Without some kind of external funding, it would almost never be worth it for any researcher to do their work. Imagine a medical researcher who is looking to study the potential benefits of a particular therapy for a kind of cancer. To work on this, she will need millions of dollars—to support herself, her research assistants, purchase lab equipment, etc. But her research will never really "pay for itself," as far as her direct interests are concerned. The chance of her getting that particular kind of cancer is rare. Maybe she might write a book for popular audiences and recuperate some money that way, but it's likely not going to cover all the costs. So, if she were left to her own devices, it would never be worth it for her to spend years and years working on the problem. Nevertheless, her research may well be tremendously valuable for the world as a whole—if she succeeds, she may save many lives. Even if her chance of finding a cure is 50/50, say, it might be worth it for society to fund her work, depending on how prevalent the cancer is. Thus, to get out of this predicament, researchers need external funding—which typically comes from governments, private donors, and tuition paying students.

But now, notice that academic research is only beneficial for society if its marginal benefits exceed marginal costs. I want to emphasize that 'marginal benefits' here is to be construed broadly—the benefits can include both the instrumental value of research (building new technologies, finding cures, etc.) as well as its intrinsic value (knowledge itself being the good in question). Presumably, research within my own field of philosophy is largely justified in the latter way: philosophers don't typically discover how to cure cancer or make smartphones or spaceships.

Clearly, not all possible research is worthwhile in the sense that the marginal benefits (broadly construed) exceed marginal costs. Here's a possible research program. The aim is to count exactly how many blades of grass there are within a large pasture in Montana. Let's say this will take a total of 1000 people working for one day, for a total expense of $500,000. Should society fund this? Of course not, it would be absurd. It's not worth spending that amount of money to figure out how many blades of grass there are in this pasture. Resources are scarce, and we should use them in better ways.

Imagine now that Bill, who is a researcher, has received a check from the government and private donors for $500,000. He could have refused the check, in which case the money would have gone to the representative sorts of things that governments and private donors fund: poverty relief, public works, art galleries, etc. Now that Bill has gotten the money, there are no strings attached, however. He can spend this money however he likes, provided it's on research. So of course, he can't just spend it on a Rolex and a yacht.

Suppose Bill can choose one of two programs. One program involves the grass counting in Montana. The other program involves looking into the environmental effects of large-scale farming. Stipulate, for simplicity, that Bill has the right training and other resources to successfully conduct either research program. It would be wrong for him to choose the former project. He'd be wasting money that could be much better used elsewhere. It seems he has a duty to pursue the latter program, even if it takes more effort, say. Part of research ethics then involves seeking projects that have a sufficiently high marginal value for society—ideally, higher than the marginal cost that society bears to fund said research.

This hypothetical is relevant to modern researchers, because we often find ourselves in exactly such a situation. For instance, consider my incentives. I receive a salary that is not conditioned upon the content of what research I pursue. I'm free to do whatever I like. Of course, I don't have tenure yet, and in order to get tenure, I will have to publish work with reputable journals and presses. But other than that, there are no content-based constraints. Now, this is the model of the humanities. The social and physical sciences work differently— the research there is often grant funded, which largely involves government agencies like the National Science Foundation awarding money for specific research projects. However, researcher professors themselves decide which projects get funded through these agencies—not on their own behalf, of course, but on behalf of others in their fields. I contend that just like Bill, individuals like me, as well as people deciding

A Duty to Speak Your Mind

59

which grant applications to fund, have a duty to see to it that the funded research is expected to have the greatest (or at least, sufficiently great) benefit *at the margins* relative to the cost.

Sometimes this might involve personal costs, though. Working on the highest value research might involve more effort or it might mean the work is harder to get published. From a narrowly self-interested perspective, of course, the thing to do for researchers is to work on the projects which yield the most publishable papers in top journals, the most opportunities for better jobs and grants etc., while requiring the least effort. If that involves counting grass, then count grass! Nonetheless, as I have been emphasizing, morality often instructs us to act contrary to our narrow self-interests, so long as the costs are not too high.

Now, in a field of inquiry that is working well, individual researchers will be incentivized to pursue those projects which in fact have the highest marginal value. Indeed, proposals to count blades of grass won't stand much chance of being funded by the National Science Foundation.

Within philosophy, I mentioned metaethics as field that is paradigmatically working well. I asked you to imagine a hypothetical situation where there were 100 naturalists and one non-naturalist in the field. Such a hypothetical situation would be unstable. Presumably there would be lots of good arguments to make for non-naturalism, which that one person hasn't formulated. This would incentivize philosophers to publish articles defending non-naturalism—there will be "low hanging fruits" to pick. And picking these fruits will be rewarded with publication in the best journals in the field. This in turn will lead to higher status and better job opportunities, and so on. A situation where only one person defends non-naturalism, then, won't last for long—in game theoretic terms, it would not be an equilibrium.[20]

Indeed, as noted previously, a wide variety of positions exist within the modern profession of metaethics, with each position having several high-profile defenders. Insofar as the total amount of money spent by society to support metaethics is warranted, then, the incentives of researchers align with the good of society. Individual researchers are incentivized to seek out projects with high marginal value. Similar points presumably apply to physics and chemistry. Researchers work on a wide range of topics and are constantly testing various hypotheses. A hypothesis that can easily be refuted won't stand unrefuted for long. A new, useful polymer that can easily be studied won't remain unstudied for long. This is not to say these three fields are working perfectly, but rather just to say they approximate the ideal.

It's helpful in this context to think of fields of inquiry as consisting of individuals harvesting a tree bearing fruit. A healthy field of inquiry will involve individuals being free to pick whichever fruit they can get their hands on. Thus, the lowest hanging fruits will be gone quickly. Eventually, the only fruits left will be high up in the tree. In contrast, an unhealthy field of inquiry might be akin to a tree where there are obstacles to picking fruit on a particular side of the tree. On such a tree, individuals will be picking fruit at ever-higher locations on one side, but on the other side, there will be fruits hanging very low, which individuals are disincentivized from picking. Yet if fruits are the goal here—as truth is presumably the goal of inquiry—then the marginal benefit to society of trying to pick the lowest fruits will be very high. Doing so won't require expensive ladders, to stretch the metaphor a bit further.

What should individual researchers do within fields where low hanging fruit are "forbidden" in the sense that picking them invites social and professional costs? Are there any such fields today? In the passage quoted in the previous chapter, Glenn Loury expresses his worry that some areas of social science are structured in this way. The worry is that there are some conclusions that most members within some fields *want* to reach, and thus there are social costs associated with conducting research whose output undermines, or provides evidence against, those conclusions.

However, if the analysis above is correct, there will be low hanging fruit to pick here *precisely because* people have been disincentivized from conducting such research. But if the work of researchers is ultimately justified in terms of what they add to the knowledge stock of humanity, as opposed to merely the status and prestige they gain for themselves, then it would seem that individual researchers have a duty to pursue such "heterodox" projects. For, the marginal benefit they provide to society is likely to be the highest if they do so.

Of course, as I have been emphasizing, the duty is a *prima facie* duty—if the costs of pursuing such research are prohibitive, then plausibly the duty fails to apply. Furthermore, the costs will often depend on the context, and in particular, the professional position of the researcher. Thus, imagine a scenario where pursuing some research projects, however well, makes Ph.D. students unemployable. Now consider a young Ph.D. student deciding what project to pursue. Morality would be too demanding if it required her to pursue research that would destroy her career.

But note that typically such costs decrease as one advances in one's career. If and when this individual gets tenure within a research university, for example, the costs of pursuing the research program in question will drop dramatically. Now that her living is secure, the brunt of the costs will involve things like social sanctions from some of her colleagues, poor luck in some of the field's top journals, etc. These costs are real—they can be unpleasant and might decrease her status. But morality sometimes demands us to do things at some cost to ourselves.

A classic historical example of someone who fulfilled this duty—or rather, went above and beyond—is Galileo Galilei. Galileo argued for the heliocentric model of the world, according to which the Earth revolves around the sun, rather than vice versa. But this was at a time in the 17th century when the Catholic Church was heavily invested in defending the opposite. Thus, the issue was not a "dry" one which people could discuss and debate openly, without cost. Ultimately, the Church found grounds for "vehement suspicion" that he defended the Copernican heliocentric model, thereby committing heresy. His *Dialogue Concerning the Two Chief World Systems* was banned and Galileo was condemned to house arrest for life. In this way, Galileo dramatically improved our understanding of the world at cost to himself.[21]

Which research invites social and professional sanction has changed over the years. We don't nowadays get worked up about what physicists find. The work of modern physicists, though fascinating, is dry in this sense. Nobody is going to get fired or put under house arrest for discovering and publishing something about black holes or neutrons. But the worry expressed by Glenn Loury, among others, is that this "dryness" is absent in some fields within social science. Defending some hypotheses, however well, invites censure, ad hominem attacks, and professional costs, according to this worry. The idea would be that as the Catholic Church was invested in particular hypotheses being true with respect to the physical world, so are the majorities within today's institutions of knowledge production invested in certain hypotheses regarding the *social* world.[22] Insofar as Loury is right, it is here that modern-day Galileos are to be found. Let me illustrate with a hypothetical example.

In the 20th century, there was a lively macroeconomic debate between the Keynesians and the Monetarists. The Keynesians believed, among other things, that during recessions, governments ought to pursue expansionary fiscal policies to stimulate the economy. Monetarists thought that such policies had no positive impact on long-term growth. Keynesians favored more flexibility for central banks, while Monetarists favored more constraints and rules on central bank actions. Each side gave various arguments and evidence for their conclusions. Today, macroeconomists draw from the insights of both sides to construct their models.

But imagine the following scenario. Imagine that in a distant possible world, the economics community was heavily invested in Monetarism being true. Journal article after journal article defended Monetarism. Monetarists received prestigious awards and university posts. But Keynesianism was verboten. A Keynesian could get an article published here and there, by stroke of luck, but it was an uphill battle. Graduate students defending Keynesianism found themselves with few job prospects. Defending Keynesianism provoked ad hominem attacks of the kind Loury describes.

What are the marginal benefits of pursuing research in such a scenario? Well, note that a good typically gets less and less valuable the more of it we have. The first article defending Monetarism is extremely beneficial. But, assuming similar quality, the 1000th article defending Monetarism will not add nearly as much. The low hanging fruit are to be found in defending Keynesianism. Moreover, given such incentive structures, our general epistemic position with respect to monetary policy will be impoverished. We just won't know if the Keynesian insights have some truth to them—because people are strongly disincentivized from voicing them!

In such a scenario, then, it is all the more important to pursue work within the Keynesian research program. By publishing the second article defending Keynesianism, you would do much more good as compared to writing the 1000th article defending the Monetarist view. In addition, even if you are a Monetarist in such a situation, you should help reduce the social and professional costs borne by the few who are defending Keynesianism, in whatever ways you can. This might involve doing your best to seek out unbiased referees for Keynesian papers as a journal editor, attempting to reduce ideological bias in hiring decisions, and so on.

The point doesn't only apply to social science, of course. Similar conclusions may be drawn with respect to the humanities. Within philosophy for instance, many careers, books, and journals are devoted to inquiry about the basic principles of justice and their application to contemporary issues. Much work in the humanities more broadly touches on social issues that are contentious and alive today, regarding which people have affective investment. But insofar as a community of academics wants to reach a particular conclusion, the worries Loury raises will be relevant. In such cases, one provides much more by way of marginal benefit by defending the heterodox side rather than piling on with the nth paper or book defending the popular conclusion.

CONCLUSION

We have a duty to preserve the health of our epistemic commons. One chief way to do so is to speak our minds despite social pressure. Social pressure distorts the evidential landscape, and so threatens the health of the epistemic commons. Hence, when we reveal our evidence to our community against countervailing pressure, we might be curing a dangerous blind spot. The duty is particularly relevant to researchers and intellectuals, given the influence they have and the social role they play. They can fulfill this duty by pursuing and encouraging others to pursue heterodox research and ideas, where there is pressure from the mainstream (relative to the context) against doing so.

An important worry this discussion raises is the question of whether individuals can make a difference. Why risk social status if all we say is going to be a proverbial "drop in the ocean" anyway? This is the topic of the next chapter. I will argue that you can often make a huge difference.

Dreading isolation more than error, they professed to share the
sentiments of the majority.
  —Alexis de Tocqueville, *The Old Regime and the Revolution*

THE INEFFICACY OBJECTION

Speaking your mind presents a collective action problem. Each
individual maximizes his narrow self-interest by not rocking
the boat—that is, only sharing evidence where there is no
social cost to doing so. But if everybody (or enough) people
act in this way, then dangerous blind spots emerge. Everyone
in the group would be better off if they all spoke their minds.

However, collective action problems, in many other domains
where there are a similarly large number of actors involved,
give rise to the *inefficacy objection*. The worry will be: whatever
you do, you're not going to make any real difference. So, you
might as well take the easy route.

Here's an example. The beef industry is a huge detriment to
the environment. A lot of land has to be cleared for pastures,
which means less forest area. Cows also require lots of food
and water, and thus meat production is not as energy efficient
as plant-based food production. Cows in particular also secrete
large quantities of methane, which is a potent greenhouse gas.
Now suppose a person enjoys eating steak, but also cares about

the environment. Giving up steak won't be that much of a sacrifice for him—he could eat fish and chicken in terms of meat instead, the production of which is less damaging to the environment. Should this person give up steak? Seems like a no-brainer to say: yes, of course.

However, he might reason thus: "I do care about environmental degradation. In an ideal world, beef consumption would be rare. But look, my consumption of steak is not going to make much of a difference. Beef farming is done on such a large scale that even if I were to completely stop now, no producer is going to raise and kill any fewer cows. They're just insensitive to my demand. If I stop eating steak, all that will happen is that I will lose out on the enjoyment I obtain from it. So, the sensible thing for me to do is to continue."

Even in cases where each individual act makes a difference, often the difference is extremely small. Thus, suppose you drive a gas guzzler instead of a hybrid vehicle. Your driving the gas guzzler is not going to make or break the ozone layer. If the ozone layer is going to be dangerously depleted, it's going to happen regardless of whether you switch to the hybrid. There are too many other actors involved. And if the ozone layer is going to be saved, your behavior in this regard is not going to stop it from being saved. So—might as well drive the gas guzzler.

Now there is a burgeoning philosophical literature on this issue.[1] Some people argue that even if you don't make a difference, your complicity in a collectively bad action is morally wrong—and so you should desist. Others argue that in many of these cases, there's a small probability that your action triggers a very bad, difference-making, outcome. Maybe eating that steak can, with a one-in-a-million chance, lead to the beef industry adding a huge new facility. This expectation, some would say, is enough for it to be the case that you shouldn't consume beef. I don't want to get into the weeds of this problem here. Rather, what I want to suggest is that the case for speaking your mind is quite different—we often *can* make a big difference. Though it may be tempting to think that one's lone voice of dissent is going to fall on deaf ears, ample psychological evidence suggests that this is often not the case.

Perhaps the most famous demonstration of this comes from Solomon Asch's experiments, conducted on college students at Swarthmore College during the 1950s.[2] Their task was simple. There were two cards. On one card was a single line. On the other card there were three lines. Subjects had to say which of the three lines on the latter card matched the length of the line on the former. Importantly, the answer was meant to be easy and obvious. As you can see in the following figure, it's *glaringly obvious* that '2' is the correct answer.

In the experimental setup, groups of seven individuals were asked to say which line matched the original, over multiple rounds with different cards. However, each group contained only one genuine test subject. The other six were confederates (i.e. actors) instructed to give canned answers. During initial rounds the confederates gave the correct answer. But on some

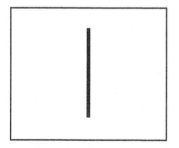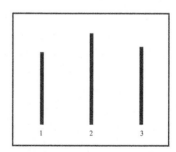

An example of line cards used in the Asch experiments[3]

rounds, the confederates unanimously gave a particular wrong answer they were instructed to give. What did the subject do in such situations? Going along with the group, 36.8% of subjects gave the wrong answer. This is fascinating from a psychological perspective because the answer was supposed to be *obvious*—indeed, removed from group settings, individuals erred less than 1% of the time. If people can be pressured to conform to the erring majority when it comes to such a simple visual question, it should not be surprising if they're often led to erring judgment on complex social issues regarding which their reference network has a strong affective investment.

What can a lone voice of sanity do in such situations? Quite a lot, apparently. The design was then manipulated so that one of the six confederates also gave the correct answer, while the others gave the same, obviously wrong, answer. In this case, the rate at which subjects went with the obviously wrong but majority-approved answer dropped by a factor of *four*. This suggests that even one dissenting voice can have a *huge* psychological impact on others. People fundamentally don't want to be *alone*.

A further finding of the experiment was that the tendency to conform differed greatly among individuals. Some (about a quarter) never conformed to the erring majority. Others went with the majority pretty much all the time, betraying the evidence of their own senses. This suggests that some individuals are more resistant to social pressures to conform—and so, if you are one of these individuals, you can make a great difference by speaking your mind.

More evidence on the effects of a single dissenter comes from studies of panels of judges.[4] It turns out that panels where every judge was appointed by one political party deliberate quite differently from panels with even a single member from

Why It's OK to Speak Your Mind

the other party. This would initially seem puzzling—the party in question has a majority in both cases, so why should such panels often reach differing conclusions? The answer is that a lone dissenter can often change the shape of deliberation by providing evidence and perspectives that would otherwise be lacking. As dramatized in the 1957 movie 12 *Angry Men*, a single person can make a big difference within group deliberation.

Of course, it would be too strong to say that every single voice can change the trajectory of the whole world. But what the social scientific research does suggest is that the lone voice can often have more influence than we give it credit for.

THE EMPEROR HAS NO CLOTHES

In Hans Christian Andersen's famous tale, "The Emperor's New Clothes," some swindlers decide to weave a new set of clothes for the very vain emperor. The catch, the swindlers say, is that fools and people not fit for his office will not be able to see them. Everyone, including the emperor, goes along with the fraud and praises the outfit. Nobody wants to be thought a fool or, particularly in the emperor's case, unfit for office. The lie ends and the bubble bursts when a child says out loud "But he hasn't got anything on."[5] Whispers travel and eventually the crowd agrees that the emperor is naked.

This story reveals a deep fact about human nature and the follies it can give rise to. What is known as *pluralistic ignorance* arises when a particular norm is actually unpopular, but widely believed to be popular. Pluralistic ignorance explains how unpopular norms can survive, often for a long time. Even if the norm is unpopular, individuals are afraid to express their discontentment because they don't want to invite social sanction. The idea of pluralistic ignorance has been used in this way to explain a range of phenomena, from the persistence of female genital cutting in parts of North Africa to the survival of unpopular governments such as the Soviet era communist regimes in Eastern Europe.[6] What ultimately matters for the persistence of a norm, then, is not whether it's popular, but rather whether it's believed to be popular.

Cristina Bicchieri lays out five conditions which facilitate pluralistic ignorance: (i) people engage in social comparison with others in their reference network, taking cues about what is to be done and said; (ii) other people's behavior is observable (in the Andersen tale, the outward praise of the Emperor's "clothes" is observable to all) and so are punishments for errant behavior; (iii) people do not express their true views out of fear of social sanction; (iv) while we think *our* outward behavior doesn't reflect our preferences, we assume that others' outward behavior *does* reveal their true preferences; and (v) we come to think that all others (or a majority) accept the norm in question.[7] What happens in such cases is that the hypothesis that the norm is unpopular is costly (or at least *appears* costly) to test. As a result, nobody tests it by airing dissent.

Furthermore, some individuals might well enforce the norm, by inflicting punishment, even as they don't accept it.[8] What better way to show that one is on the good side than punishing or calling out others? Thus, someone wanting to display loyalty to an authoritarian regime which he internally dislikes might nonetheless report his neighbor for complaining about the rations. Presumably, these are among the worst characters in such a situation. For, not only do they manifest hypocrisy and inauthenticity, but there's also a callous infliction of often significant punishment for a small benefit to oneself—and all in the service of a norm that by their own lights is not worthwhile.

Pluralistic ignorance has enormous implications for how we should think of the utility of an individual's speaking her mind. As Bicchieri emphasizes, an unpopular norm can become pervasive through the actions of very few trendsetters. A vocal minority that is willing and able to punish dissenters can induce compliance from a much larger population. Importantly, this punishment need not be legal or physical. It may take the form of purely social sanction: public denouncement, calls for dissociation, etc. Even purely social pressures can cause a spiral of silence, where nobody dares to question certain assumptions or voice certain opinions—particularly on social and political matters. Fear of isolation is a powerful motive in human psychology, and so most individuals, when they *perceive* some opinion to be widespread and passionately held, are likely to suppress their own hesitation about it.[9]

However, the bright side is that just as it takes only a few to bring such norms into place, a few individuals—or even one—can burst the bubble. This is precisely what happens in Andersen's tale: a young child, oblivious to the concerns and reasoning of the adults, speaks her mind. As a result, the bubble bursts—people realize that it's not just them who see no clothes on the emperor. Thus, "when a norm is the result of pluralistic ignorance," Bicchieri says, "it may take very little to subvert it."[10] If a norm exists due to pluralistic ignorance, the conditions are already there for it to quickly collapse. The norm exists only because individuals widely believe that the norm is widely endorsed. What is thus needed is reliable information that the norm is in fact *not* widely endorsed. Often, an open dissenting voice can allow people to make that inference: "it's not only I who think this; there must be lots of others." Alternatively, opinion polling released by a trusted agency showing that the norm is not widely held can undermine its power.

Regardless, the actions of a few, and sometimes even the lone individual, can matter quite a lot.

PARTISAN DISPUTES

Our age is marked by disagreement that is notoriously partisan. This is obviously not an anomaly. History is littered with cases of separate ideological factions struggling for power and influence. Witness the *stasis* experienced by ancient Greek city-states, or the religious wars in Europe before the 1648 Peace of Westphalia, or the Spanish Civil War of the 20th century. Nonetheless, perhaps our time exhibits more by way of polarization as compared with the past few decades, at least in the West.

Partisan strife invites the following challenge for the utility of speaking one's mind. On the issues that form the basis of partisan dispute, the different sides are already entrenched. Someone might thus think, "I have evidence and arguments regarding some of these issues. But if I disagree with my friends or colleagues, that will hurt my social relationships. And given how entrenched people are, nobody is going to change their minds anyway. So, what's the point in me voicing my thoughts?"

Two points are noteworthy here. One is that the distribution of public opinion may often look more polarized than it actually is. Partisans or activists on either side of the debate will have an incentive to formulate the issue as a disagreement between two extremes. So, this might create a situation where the loudest voices are the polarized ones. However, it can often be the case that many or even most individuals favor a moderate position.[11] Hence, even though by being a moderate, one is likely to get attacked by both extremes, one might still be making a valuable contribution to the discourse in general.

Secondly, even if by voicing an opinion or perspective one doesn't budge entrenched partisans, moderates may well find the idea illuminating. The main point of expressing dissent or a new perspective within a politicized or polarized environment, then, is *not* to change the views of entrenched partisans. John Stuart Mill put it thus:

> I acknowledge that the tendency of all opinions to become sectarian is not cured by the freest discussion, but is often heightened and exacerbated thereby; the truth which ought to have been, but was not, seen, being rejected all the more violently because proclaimed by persons regarded as opponents. But it is not on the impassioned partisan, it is on the calmer and more disinterested bystander, that this collision of opinions works its salutary effects.[12]

The challenge from the perspective of individual expression, of course, is that the "calmer and more disinterested bystander" is not likely to voice her assent publicly. The "impassioned partisan," on the other hand, is likely to voice his censure publicly. And so there can be this filtering mechanism by which only a subset of the reactions to our ideas are conveyed to us. Hence, it can seem as though we're not making any difference even if we actually are.

NOBLE LIES

I have been defending a *prima facie* duty to share one's evidence in the face of social pressure. A common refrain here, however, is that some evidence is such that it can only do harm to society if shared. Perhaps bad elements will use the evidence for nefarious ends. Perhaps the evidence will cause unnecessary offense.

Now, as clarified in the previous chapter, the duty to share evidence against social pressure only kicks in on matters likely to be of broad epistemic importance. In other words, the relevant question is: does the evidence bear on our general understanding of the world, in significant ways? I am defending the somewhat radical view that if the answer to this question is yes, then there is an imperfect duty to share the evidence. The duty doesn't kick in when the matter does not have sufficiently broad epistemic significance. Thus, you don't have a duty to say out loud in your grandma's presence that the sweater she knitted for you is not your style. The matter is about as insignificant as it gets from the perspective of our collective epistemic commons.

In contrast, the scientific contributions of Galileo are on the other end of the spectrum. They fundamentally changed our picture of the physical world. If we still thought the sun goes around the Earth, our view of the world would be deeply impoverished. And on the practical side, presumably science and technology couldn't have progressed to where they are now if nobody were allowed to profess heliocentrism.

But now of course we can imagine what someone sympathetic to the Church might have said in Galileo's time. A common (and natural) worry then had been: if the Earth is round and spinning, why don't objects fly off rather than remain stationary? The theory would have seemed outlandish to people given their experience with the physical world. Why risk the potential undermining of people's faith in the Church, just so someone can propound this crazy view? After all, this faith is essential for avoiding eternal damnation. In addition, faith is important for social cohesion. So, the upside is small and the downside is huge! Of course, removed as we are from that time, such reasoning will have little grip on us, and we'll be tempted to dismiss it as silly and outdated. But if we genuinely try to place ourselves in the shoes of the average person or clergyman at the time, the reasoning is not so foreign. The persecutors of Galileo were just people like us; we're not some kind of angel compared to them.

My point is that each age has its imaginative limitations. From the perspective of a particular age, the epistemic and practical benefits of a purportedly heretical theory will not be obvious. Individuals in Galileo's time could not have even conceived of the perspective that modern physics gives us. They could not have imagined that humans in large metal objects would eventually travel to the moon or that people would communicate from across the world by using devices that bounce signals off of satellites orbiting the Earth. Moreover, people *wanted* to believe that the Earth was at the center of the universe—it wasn't a "dry" matter to them. They were hugely invested in the notion, given religious interpretation at the time, that Earth was a special place, carefully put in the center of creation by a watchful God, as opposed to just a random planet orbiting a random star.[13]

But we, even now, are far from dispassionate and omniscient. Just as people were blinded by ideology and lack of imagination in the 17th century, so can we be similarly blinded. Hence, we should be very humble about our ability to determine which pieces of evidence, insofar as they concern matters of great epistemic importance, are better kept suppressed.

Furthermore, when people make claims about particular bits of evidence or forms of inquiry being best left suppressed, what justifies their confidence? Being able to justifiably believe such claims would seem to require some kind of multiple regression analysis, or better yet, a randomized control trial—that's how we do good social science. Perhaps some set of societies allows for open inquiry into matter X, while another set, roughly on par with respect to various indicators, doesn't. If the latter eventually ended up being better off along various dimensions of importance, then it might be concluded that X is best left untouched. But notice that such analyses are not (and often cannot be) conducted, and so the claim that X is best left untouched is meant to be taken on faith or intuition. The sorts of evidence that would justify belief in such claims, then, are conspicuously absent. It's therefore difficult not to suspect that efforts to make particular forms of evidence and inquiry verboten are actually efforts to protect an ideology that some have affective or political investment in, whose foundations are shaky—much like the agents of the Church in Galileo's time.

In addition, the nobility of lies is extremely context dependent. When the context changes, a lie that once looked noble might become very dangerous. Thus, for example, imagine an ancient village which believes that a particular tree is sacred.[14] Perhaps this belief allows for social cohesion and group loyalty. Maybe these bonds are important enough for the flourishing of the village that one might think people raising doubts about the sacredness of the tree do the village a disservice. The sacredness of the tree then, though a lie, is a perhaps a *noble* lie.

But now imagine that the context changes. Decades of peace are disturbed by impending conflict. Imagine that a powerful army now seeks to come and destroy the village. The sacred tree, however, stands in the middle of the village and will get desecrated and burned down. The villagers have enough advance notice that they can take their important belongings and flee into the mountains, where they will be safe. Alternatively, they can stand and defend the sacred tree. The noble lie can turn dangerous in this way if it skews the villagers' deliberation in favor of defending the tree—they will probably all get killed and nothing good will come of it. The tree is just a tree after all, and the villagers' lives are more valuable. If the nobility of lies is heavily context dependent in this way, it's perhaps best to avoid them, or at least treat them as pleasant fictions in the back of our minds.

Some of these points perhaps find their best expression in Mill. He says, referring to what I have been calling noble lies:

> It is also often argued, and still oftener thought, that none but bad men would desire to weaken these salu-tary beliefs . . . But those who thus satisfy themselves, do not perceive that the assumption of infallibility is merely shifted from one point to another. The usefulness of an opinion is itself matter of opinion: as disputable, as open to discussion, and requiring discussion as much, as the opinion itself.[15]

Even regarding matters thought by a particular age or society to be noxious and rightly forbidden, then, the heretic performs an extremely valuable service for society. Hence, the imperfect duty I have been defending applies in this case as well, and it is perhaps all the more important to fulfill it in such contexts, so long as the costs to oneself are not too severe.

Now, some will quickly admit that many (or most) soci-eties in the past were radically wrong about which pieces of evidence or which arguments were dangerous. But they might say that we, now, have a roughly good grasp on what's best left unsaid. But notice how odd it would be to think that this age and *this cultural context* is infallible in its judgment about such matters. "All human societies in the past have erred, but we are absolutely right," is an attitude that, though implicit and pervasive, upon reflection merits incredulity. What a convenient denial of basic inductive reasoning! In this vein, Mill writes: "Yet it is as evident in itself as any amount of argument can make it, that ages are no more infallible than individuals; every age having held many opinions which subsequent ages have deemed not only false but absurd; and it is as certain that many opinions, now general, will be rejected by future ages, as it is that many, once general, are rejected by the present."[16]

The temptation here is to think that yes, our zeitgeist might be mistaken about a few peripheral things, but eventually we'll inevitably make progress. Nonetheless, we should be aware of the possibility that what looks like progress might actually be a regress, and that the zeitgeist is mistaken not simply on peripheral matters, but in its most fundamental assumptions. The historical record gives us very strong inductive evidence for worrying about this. As Mill says, "History teems with instances of truth put down by persecution. If not suppressed for ever, it may be thrown back for centuries."[17] If this is right, then the dissenter is a crucial element in all eras, not just past ones.

AGGRESSIVE CONFORMISM AND GRANDSTANDING

Consider the following character: the *aggressive conformist*.[18] The aggressive conformist seeks to one-up the other members of his social group by going even further in the direction his group is going. In this way, he seeks to display that he is committed to the values of the group much more than the other, ordinary members. The regular conformist simply wants to avoid sticking out and making waves, thus avoiding possible social sanction. The aggressive conformist, on the other hand, actively seeks out further social status by going above and beyond, as it were. One way in which aggressive conformism might manifest itself is via punishment of dissenters. Punishing dissenters is an excellent way to demonstrate one's commitment to the values of the group, and can be rewarded with social status. Another manifestation of aggressive conformism might be what philosophers Justin Tosi and Brandon Warmke call *moral grandstanding*.

Grandstanding, in their analysis, is the use of moral talk for self-promotion. To grandstand is to make claims about justice or morality driven primarily by the desire to be thought of as morally exemplary by others. Tosi and Warmke give the following example of grandstanding, which they call "ramping up":

> Ann: We can all agree that the Senator's behavior was wrong and that she should be publicly censured.
>
> Ben: Oh please—if we really cared about justice we should seek her removal from office. We simply cannot tolerate that sort of behavior and I will not stand for it.
>
> Chip: As someone who has long fought for social justice, I'm sympathetic to these suggestions, but does anyone know the criminal law on this issue? I want to suggest that we should pursue criminal charges. We would all do well to remember that the world is watching.[19]

What we see in effect is a *moral arms race*. Social status is a zero-sum game. If I have more, that means others must have less. Social status is status relative to other members of a particular group. And so, if the goal is to gain social status, the thing to do is to try and show why one is more exemplary relative to some set of standards the group implicitly or explicitly endorses, as compared to others in the relevant group.

Now, the Senator's behavior in the above case may well be wrong. But what's fascinating here are the motives of the actors and the dynamics of their conversation. Once Ann says the Senator is wrong, the gauntlet has been thrown down. Now if Ben and Chip just concur, they don't establish themselves as morally exemplary or special. Everyone would just be at the same level. So, they don't simply agree and nod their heads. Ben goes further than Ann—he, apparently, is more morally upstanding than Ann now. Ann only saw that the Senator's behavior is wrong. But Ben realizes, given the paragon of moral virtue that he is, that the senator must, in addition, be removed. And for the same reason, Chip adds to this by going even further—he's even better than Ben.[20]

We have all seen this type of behavior, particularly in online discussion. What is of interest for our purposes is that it would be a bad implication of the view presented here if it yields that Ben and Chip are speaking their minds in a virtuous way. Fortunately, this is not an implication. For, when we assess virtue, motives matter. The aggressive conformist is primarily motivated by winning the zero-sum game of social status. Like the contrarian or the troll, he is not motivated by promoting the health of the epistemic commons or trying to reach the truth on some issue. Secondly, the aggressive conformist is not acting *against* social pressure. There's no cost (narrowly construed) for the aggressive conformist in doing what he does. Rather, at least as far as he can tell, his words and actions are going to be rewarded with *more* social status in the group.

Nonetheless, the aggressive conformist does present us with a challenge: namely, of considering whether and to what extent people can intentionally fulfill the duty presented here.

The problem is that the aggressive conformist will rarely if ever think of himself as such. Such a person will likely see himself as the brave soul fighting for justice, even if he is, deep down, an avid seeker of social status. And so, the risk is that from the vantage point of the aggressive conformist, he is already bravely speaking his mind. The duty to speak your mind against social pressure, then, seems like it would be harder to follow than the duty not to break promises or the duty not to lie. It's generally pretty easy to tell (though even here, we are often capable of great self-deception) whether we're lying or breaking a promise. But it would seem harder to tell whether we are speaking our minds against social pressure. And so, the ideal I am defending here risks being one that we can't follow.

Indeed, decades of social scientific research show that we humans are very good at deceiving ourselves about our motives and avoiding cognitive dissonance.[21] We rationalize our actions to present them in the best light. If our actions conflict with our stated ideals, we try to reinterpret the situation so as to suppress the conflict. And if our publicly stated opinions don't match our private beliefs initially, we try to bring the latter closer to the former, all the while deceiving ourselves about the social, as opposed to the truth-sensitive, nature of our reasons for coming to believe them. Surprisingly, this phenomenon tends to occur *more* if the rewards for stating a particular opinion are *small*. Thus, a person who says something merely to get praise from his peers in the form of social media "likes," say, is more likely to come to *really* believe that thing as opposed to the person who pays lip service to a belief system in order to avoid jail or execution.[22]

We do all this in part because, as George Orwell has the protagonist eventually come to realize in the novel 1984, "if you want to keep a secret, you must also hide it from yourself."[23] If we don't paint ourselves in a flattering light, we risk presenting ourselves to others in a non-flattering light. And that is dangerous, especially in the context of our evolutionary past. A selfish, non-cooperative person would have risked being ostracized by the tribe, and ostracism often meant death. We thus have very strong tendencies to seek the approval of others. And people want to cooperate with other cooperators, not egoistic freeloaders.[24] Hence, we are experts at presenting— both to ourselves and to others—what are at bottom egoistic, selfish motives, as being selfless and other-regarding. This is in fact what the aggressive conformist does. Chip, in Tosi and Warmke's example, will likely not see himself as vying for social status—even if that is what he is doing. Rather, he will see himself as bravely fighting for justice.

Thus, in many cases, it will be hard to tell if we're just vying for status or actually speaking our minds despite social pressure not to. But here's perhaps a rule of thumb. *If saying something gets you showered in praise by members of your reference network— the group whose approval matters to your social and professional life—you're likely vying for social status rather than speaking your mind.* Thus, consider a person who writes a post on social media couched in the language of conviction and bravery. Suppose also that most of his friends or followers on the platform are representative of his reference network—they are colleagues, real-life friends, members of the profession he works in, etc. Now imagine the post gets hundreds of likes, with scores of comments chiming in to agree with the sentiment, perhaps even commending the bravery of writing the post. Such a person is vying for status, no matter what he tells himself. He is simply not speaking his mind against the social pressure.

Now of course, sometimes a person bursting a bubble of pluralistic ignorance may get showered with praise. We can imagine this happening to the child in Andersen's fairy tale. "Thanks for saying out loud what we were all thinking!" some people might say. But this will not be the case with the all-too-common pattern of behavior described above. In such cases, many in the social network will be saying similar things. The aggressive conformist will be trying to express even more outrage or even harsher condemnation or even loftier praise with regards to some social or political matter. This kind of behavior is manifestly not some courageous bursting of a bubble of pluralistic ignorance. It is straightforward social status seeking, albeit veiled in noble motives.

Four

> It is astonishing what foolish things one can temporarily believe
> if one thinks too long alone.
>
> —John Maynard Keynes, *The General Theory*

SPEAKING YOUR MIND—FOR YOURSELF OR OTHERS?

So far, I have been defending a duty to speak your mind (more precisely: to share evidence you have despite countervailing social pressure) as a way to serve humanity. Dissenters perform a crucial service to society by alleviating its blind spots. Blind spots can not only warp our understanding of the world, which is bad in itself, but can also have terrible practical consequences. Conformism then is akin to free riding on the work of dissenters—dissenters bear the costs of speaking up but conformists reap the benefits without paying any cost of their own. The conformist is like the roommate who never does the dishes, expecting others to pick up after him.

But serving others is not the only reason to speak your mind. In fact, I will now argue, speaking your mind is essential to flourishing as a human being. Therefore, you should speak your mind not only as a service to *others*, but also as a service to *yourself*.

However, this might seem like a self-contradiction. For, in previous chapters I said that we should speak our minds *despite* costs to ourselves. But then is this not an admission that speaking your mind against social pressure is detrimental to one's well-being? Speaking our minds may well be beneficial to the epistemic commons, but it might seem hard to pretend that it's good for us. Rather, we promote our own self-interest if we go with the flow. This way, we don't bear the social and professional costs that may be associated with speaking our minds.

Now, of course it is hard to deny that speaking your mind can sometimes go against your self-interest. Here's a paradigm case: consider a dissenter under Stalin's reign of terror. She believes that despite the many social and economic problems that existed then, life was better before the 1917 Russian Revolution. But if the dissenter says what she thinks about why collectivized farming or forced labor camps are a bad idea, she will be tortured and executed. Manifestly then, the dissenter's speaking her mind is bad insofar as her interests are concerned.

Extreme cases notwithstanding though, often it is necessary, as a general matter, to bear some costs in order to promote one's own overall self-interest. Similarly, I will be arguing, it can often be the case that speaking your mind and inviting social costs can nonetheless be important for your flourishing as a human being.

This might seem absurd, but it is not. Consider a simple example. There are lots of costs associated with exercising regularly. First of all, there is the time involved—an opportunity cost. In the hour it takes to get ready, stretch, line up a podcast, go to the gym, and then shower afterwards, you could have been doing something else. Furthermore, exercising is often unpleasant—pushing yourself on that last rep or keeping a good running pace is *painful*. But nobody would conclude from this that exercising regularly is bad for you.

It's a mundane fact of life that we have to bear some costs along some dimensions to reap greater benefits along others. Studying for the LSAT may not be fun, but you should do it if you want to get into a good law school within the United States. Some people may not like the taste of green vegetables, but they should eat them nonetheless. Cleaning your room is tedious and boring compared to watching TV—but it's a bad idea to never pick up and organize your surroundings. If we always took the easiest, most comfortable option every step of the way, we'd lead short, stunted, and frustrated lives.

The following worry may linger, however. In the cases above, delayed gratification leads to tangible benefits. Exercising is painful, but you will likely experience more pleasure and avoid painful conditions in the long run if you do regularly exercise. For instance, you will lessen the risk of osteoporosis and heart disease, both unpleasant affairs. Exercise also gives you a pleasurable buzz for the rest of the day, and has lots of benefits with regards to improving moods and reducing depression. Similarly, eating vegetables lets you avoid physical pain due to bad health in the long run. Or consider studying for the LSAT. Yes, it is boring and tedious now, but it will improve your odds of eventually getting into a good law school. And getting into a good law school will be good for your social status—it will mean a greater chance of working at a prestigious law firm with a good salary. It might also mean greater respect and praise from family and friends.

But what about speaking your mind? What's the analogous payoff? Remember that speaking your mind *against* social pressure by stipulation invites social cost. Of course, speaking your mind insofar as your mind aligns with the opinions approved by your social group will not have adverse consequences in this way. On the contrary, it will often garner you praise. But that's not the subject matter of this book—rather, I have been at pains to defend sharing one's evidence *precisely when* there are social costs involved. What could possibly be the upside there?

Here are some reasons to suspect that there is often no upside. Speaking your mind on a topic when there is countervailing social pressure will come with substantial costs, particularly, the potential for isolation. People within your social circle might distance themselves from you, whether subtly or explicitly. Some may admire your courage secretly, but not show it. Remember, if too many people overtly admire your courage within your social network, you're probably not displaying any genuine courage.

Now, of course, a distinct social circle may appreciate what you say, but if they're not the group that matters for your standing in society, then it is of little comfort. Thus, suppose an idea is taboo among young professionals. It is of little comfort for a young professional to be told that many rural farmers agree with her opinion. The farmers are not going to be the ones inviting her to parties or giving her raises. They may also not be fun or practical for her to hang out with, apart from the context of an occasional trip to the countryside. Her world is markedly different from theirs. And what's more, just as she disagrees with her milieu on some things, she might disagree with the farmers on others—what then? She would just be substituting one set of things she's not supposed to say for another. What's more, it is psychologically costly to exit one social network and ensconce oneself within another in this way, even when it is possible.

So much for the possible negatives. On the other hand, the positive upshots insofar as your well-being is concerned are hard to locate. Here's one possibility. Maybe you go against the grain but are ultimately vindicated. Say ten years later it turns out you were right. Is this sufficient recompense? For two main reasons, the answer typically will be no. First, your social standing may well have deteriorated during those ten years such that the praise you might receive afterwards pales in comparison. Second, people often forget who said what. Others, indeed even the very people who inflicted the social costs on you, might reposition themselves so as to either downplay their past opinions or simply deny they had them. They might even claim they were right all along. Being wrong in this way often carries little cost, and being right carries little benefit for the individual. Thus, it might seem that even if speaking your mind is a morally praiseworthy act, it cannot be good from a purely *prudential* point of view. Whatever it may be that morality recommends in this regard, prudence recommends conformity.

Now, some people have particularly weighty *expressive needs*.[1] That is, they find it very unsettling to suppress their thoughts and opinions. They have a strong desire to express their ideas, and social pressure feels unusually oppressive to them. Maybe such people should speak their minds, for their own sakes, to some extent. They might often feel better getting the load off their chest, even if there are some associated social costs. Speaking your mind, then, may be like relieving an itch, if you are one of these people. Go ahead and scratch, if it's bothering you so much. But if scratching is going to reopen a wound, try to resist the urge. Focus your attention on something else, go distract yourself. Try to put on a soothing lotion. Similarly, if the projected social costs are going to outweigh the satisfaction that you might feel for saying your piece, control yourself—don't say your piece. Go watch a movie or something. At least for your own sake, that is.

This reasoning is natural and tempting. However, it all assumes that pleasure, pain, and social status are the only things that matter in life. I am happy to concede that if what you want in life primarily is social or professional status, or the warm glow of being praised by others, you shouldn't speak your mind. If *that* is what makes life valuable, then by all means conform away—unless, that is, you are convinced by the other-regarding reasons described in earlier chapters.

Below, I draw upon ancient Greek philosophy to claim that pleasure or status are not what make life fundamentally worth living. One positive answer we get from the ancient Greeks is that a good life consists in the excellent use of our rational capacities. But in order to achieve this, I will argue, you must speak your mind.

For the purposes of this chapter, speaking your mind involves not only sharing your evidence, which was the subject matter of Chapter 2, but also asking questions, raising doubts, and considering alternatives. Nonetheless, speaking your mind does involve going against social pressure in some way. Making a mundane comment about the day's weather or saying something that your reference network encourages you to say does not amount to "speaking your mind," in the sense relevant here. Furthermore, the requirement of engaging in good faith is still crucial, as before.

REASON AND HUMAN FLOURISHING

What makes a life well-lived? A tempting answer is the maximal presence of pleasure and the minimal presence of pain. The idea would be that the best lived lives are those with the most pleasures and the least pains.

But it seems that this can't be right upon reflection. Imagine an offer to live the rest of your life on a beach resort, full of whatever kinds of pleasures you seek. That would be great for a while no doubt. But if your life was to be limited to the pleasures—the piña coladas, the sexual adventures, the TV—wouldn't you get bored? Wouldn't you itch to do something meaningful? Maybe you could keep it up for a few months, but I imagine that such a life would eventually bring about ennui and existential dread for many people. Now, you might say that if such a life brings ennui, then it is ipso facto not pleasurable. And so, I have not shown that the most pleasurable life is also not the best.

Yet, such thought experiments do reveal something important—what we ultimately seek is *meaning* not pleasure. Pleasure may well be a concomitant of a meaningful life, but a meaningful life is not one that is organized primarily around getting pleasure. The 19th century German philosopher Friedrich Nietzsche put it thus: "If we have our own why of life, we will put up with almost any how. Man does not seek pleasure; only the Englishman does."[2] The jab at Englishmen here is directed at hedonistic utilitarianism, which had gained prominence within British philosophy at the time. In particular, Jeremy Bentham popularized the idea that pleasure and pain are the only things that matter morally. Nietzsche's point is that we are fundamentally meaning-seeking creatures, not pleasure-seeking ones.

The ancient Greek philosophers also emphasized that pleasure is not the ultimate goal of life. Aristotle says early on in his *Nicomachean Ethics*: "The many, the most vulgar, would seem to conceive the good and happiness as pleasure, and hence they also like the life of gratification. In this they appear completely slavish, since the life they decide on is a life for grazing animals."[3] The idea here is that a life oriented towards pleasure would underemphasize the exercise of those capacities that make us distinctively human. Even cows and rabbits can experience gustatory and sexual pleasure. Of course, this is not to say we should avoid such pleasures; rather the point is that what makes a life well-lived is the proper exercise of our distinctively human capacities.

Aristotle's argument for this is that when we talk about good objects in general, we appeal to their characteristic work (*ergon*). Thus, a good knife is one that cuts well. A good shoe is one that protects our feet well—it doesn't flake off, has a sole that is hard enough, and so on. A good table is sturdy and has a large enough surface area. Note that in all these cases, we apply the predicate 'good' depending on the kind of object we're looking at. What makes a knife good is thus not what makes a table or shoe good. In order to find out what the good of a knife is, we have to figure out what makes it distinctive relative to other objects. In the case of knives, this is easy enough: knives are objects designed by humans to fulfill a particular function, namely, cutting.[4]

But Aristotle thought this kind of reasoning could illuminate how we should think of good human lives as well. In order to figure out what a well-lived human life consists in, he thought, we have to look at what is distinctive and special about humans. What is it that is special about humans, when we look around at the rest of the animal kingdom and inanimate reality? It's not the ability to feel pleasure—cows and giraffes can feel it too. It's not the ability to see, hear, digest, grow tall, etc., either. Rather, what's special about humans is their ability to *reason*. A good human life then, is one that exhibits the excellent exercise of our reasoning capabilities, over the course of a reasonably complete life.[5]

Just as Aristotle rejects pleasure as the aim of a good life, he rejects status-seeking. He says:

> The cultivated people . . . conceive the good as honor . . . This, however, appears to be too superficial to be what we are seeking; for it seems to depend more on those who honor than on the honored, whereas we intuitively believe that the good is something of our own and hard to take from us. Further, it would seem, they pursue honor to convince themselves that they are good; at any rate, they seek to be honored by prudent people, among people who know them, and for virtue. It is clear, then, that—in their view at any rate—virtue is superior to honor.[6]

The thought here is that upon reflection, what we can endorse as a well-lived life might well contain status and prestige, but these things should reflect our good qualities and achievements. Consider the Nobel Prize. An accomplished economist might look at her achievement of the Nobel with great pride, but she will be proud of it *qua* recognition of her work in economics. *That*, fundamentally, is what she is rightly proud of—and she is happy that her peers and the international community have recognized it as such. Contrast this case with someone whose only goal is to win the Nobel. From early in his career, he has organized his research program so as to maximize the chance of receiving the prize. He sees any work he does merely as a means to one day receiving the Nobel Prize and the recognition of his peers and the newspapers. Such an attitude would seem distorted and perverse—indeed, superficial as Aristotle says.

Again, none of this is to say that we should avoid pleasure or status. It's not to say you should never get that relaxing massage or watch a fun movie. Neither is it to say you should reject promotions or the Nobel Prize. Rather, we should keep in mind that pleasure and status are goods that are subordinate to the ultimate goal of life. One way to think about it is the following. If we never treat ourselves to human pleasures we might get stressed, dejected, or lonely. This in turn will likely impede our ability to achieve meaningful goals. Similarly, prestige and status bring along with them an enhanced ability to do our work. You will likely not have the time or energy or publishing connections to write a proper scholarly book if you don't have a job at a university. Or, you might not get to bring your innovative product idea to fruition if you don't receive some initial funding from venture capital. These things require some prestige and status within the respective professions. But it's a mistake to lose sight of these things for what they are: means for achieving our ends, not ends-in-themselves.[7]

All this is of course easy to assent to in the abstract. When the rubber meets the road, we're often tempted to seek status at the expense of doing good work, or seek the pleasure that comes with social praise at the expense of being authentic. But of course, temptation and self-deception are part and parcel of human life. Thus, achieving the good life is not easy—but isn't that as it should be?

REASONING AND SPEAKING YOUR MIND

According to Aristotle, a good human life consists in the excellent exercise of our capacity to reason, over the course of a full enough life. What are the implications for speaking your mind? Here, I will argue that speaking your mind is *essential* for developing your rational capacities. The core idea is that we are social creatures in a fundamental sense: our reasoning capacities themselves are essentially social. We reason by talking with others and bouncing ideas back and forth. We do not and cannot reason well in isolation. Therefore, in order to properly develop our rational capacities, we must express our ideas to others. Otherwise, we will remain stunted and deformed as rational creatures. The good life then, if it consists in the proper development and exercise of our rational capacities, must involve speaking our minds.

Against this notion, one might raise the following worry. Outward expression may well be important for getting people to hear what we say, or promoting our interests. It can be crucial for lobbying the government, starting a revolution, getting appreciated for our thoughts and creativity, forming and maintaining relationships, and a host of other things. But how could it be important for developing as a thinker? To develop as a thinker, isn't it sufficient to, well . . . think? Speaking your mind, after all, can only occur *after* you have done the thinking; and so, thinking is prior to speaking, not vice versa. But if thinking is prior to speaking, then speaking your mind cannot be fundamentally important for developing as a thinker. Of course, this is not to say that you can think well in complete isolation from others. We need others to help us develop as thinkers. But that's what reading, listening to lectures, and the like are for. We can develop well as thinkers if we do things like reading good books, paying attention to lectures from good teachers, and processing and thinking through the issues for ourselves. Outward expression is neither here nor there insofar as thinking well is concerned.

But this flies in the face of what every teacher knows all too well. You can't get students to understand physics, for example, by simply having them read a textbook. Maybe this would be possible for some aliens in a distant galaxy, but it is not possible for humans. Not only is passively reading formulas not enough for gaining understanding in physics, neither is looking at problems solved by others. The only way to gain understanding is by *working on problems yourself*. There's simply no substitute for getting out a pen and paper (or tablet etc.) and trying to solve the problems. It's an exceedingly routine experience to read through a chapter, think you understand the material, and then realize you don't really understand as soon as you try to solve one of the exercises in the back. The same is true for mathematics, chemistry, etc.

Further, it's not only the technical fields that have this feature. The only way to do philosophy well, for instance, is by actually talking to others and writing. Simply reading and passively consuming the material is not enough. Often, we think we understand why an argument is wrong, but then struggle to formulate the issue when writing it down. It can take considerable effort even to describe the author's argument in the first place. Understanding, then, seems to require outward expression for us humans. Feedback is crucial as well. It's not possible to develop into a good physicist or philosopher without some feedback from teachers and peers. Maybe they will correct a mistake we make. Or maybe they will allow us to view the subject matter in a new, more illuminating way than we had been. Good teachers thus emphasize practice and feedback, whatever their subject matter may be.

Feedback is a deep feature of learning. When a child is learning how to walk, its motor system is constantly incorporating feedback from experience—falling, stumbling, bumping into something—in all kinds of subtle ways. The same thing goes when someone learns how to ride a bicycle. You can't learn to ride a bicycle by reading a book. Feedback—i.e. what made you fall, veer off, etc.—is essential. When computer scientists created the artificial intelligence that could beat human players in the complex game of Go, they did so by "training" the system through millions of games with itself. Over time, the AI developed a sense of which moves are "good," based on its past experience of what worked and what didn't.[8] Even artificial intelligence, then, requires feedback for learning. We humans, of course, can't receive this feedback (except in a very attenuated sense) by simply talking to ourselves. That's not . . . how we're built. We need feedback to come from others. But then in order to get that feedback we need to communicate with others, whether it be through speaking, writing, or something else.

In her original and illuminating defense of free speech, philosopher Seana Shiffrin offers what she calls a "thinker-based" approach to understanding the role of legal protections for self-expression. Her core idea is that provisions like the First Amendment are principally justified because they are indispensable to the development of individuals as thinkers. In other words, we can't properly develop as thinkers unless we are able to speak freely. While the purpose of this book is not primarily to defend the legal protection of free speech, Shiffrin's analysis is germane here because it sheds light on why outward expression is essential for the inward development of our rational capacities.

Shiffrin observes that we have several interests as thinkers. They include: developing our capacities for theoretical and practical reasoning, coming to know the truth on a variety of matters, using our imaginations, developing our moral agency, becoming unique individuals, being authentic, living among others as the unique individuals we are, and being recognized by others as being the individuals we are.[9] She then argues that these interests we have as thinkers can only be satisfied under a regime of free speech, where dissenting opinions are not legally punished.

On the need for outward expression in developing our thinking, she writes:

> one cannot fully develop a complex mental world, identify its contents, evaluate them, and distinguish between those that are merely given and those one endorses, unless one has the ability to externalize bits of one's mind, formally distance those bits from one's mind, identify them as particulars, and then evaluate them to either endorse, reject, or modify them. For many people, some thoughts may only be fully identified and known to themselves if made linguistically or representationally explicit. Many find that difficult to do using merely mental language, especially when it comes to sufficiently complex ideas; one has to externalize his or her thoughts through oral or written speech or through other forms of symbolic representation to form or identify them completely. Only then is it possible to evaluate their contents . . . Of course, it isn't merely the development and identification of one's thoughts that requires the use of representation and external articulation. To pursue our interest in forming true beliefs about ourselves and our environment, we need the help of others' insights and beliefs, as well as their reactions and evaluative responses to our beliefs.[10]

Shiffrin corroborates her view by noting what happens to people in solitary confinement. Prisoners subjected to such isolation are known to suffer devastating mental deterioration, often experiencing hallucination and psychosis. Losing social contact with others, along with the ability to receive feedback from them on our perception of reality, makes us lose touch with reality itself.[11] Shiffrin acknowledges that prisoners in solitary confinement lose more than just their ability to interact with others—they also lose their freedom to move beyond a confined space or eat what they want, among other things. However, this is also true of prison inmates in general, and yet most such inmates do not experience the sorts of breakdown that affect those in isolation.

Now, Shiffrin's point is not that being unable to speak our minds is on par with solitary confinement. Rather, she wants to claim that the setback involved lies along the same spectrum; being unable to say what you really think is a mild version of the kind of problem that total isolation brings. Being unable to speak your mind is akin to being locked in a *mental* prison, with nobody to share your thoughts with.

For our purposes, the important point is that just as our rational capacities break down or become severely stunted and deformed in solitary confinement, so do they fail to flourish if we don't speak our minds. Of course, in the latter case the degradation is not nearly as severe, but it is there nonetheless. Importantly, these things lie on a spectrum: someone who cannot or will not speak his mind in most circumstances, except with regards to trivial matters, suffers more with regard to the development and exercise of his rational capacities than another person who often speaks her mind but holds back on certain matters so as to avoid the big-ticket social costs. Likewise, the typical resident of North Korea suffers more vis-à-vis being locked in a mental prison, so to speak, than the average person living in a modern democracy; meanwhile, someone locked up in solitary confinement suffers more in this respect than either of these cases. Presumably, this is not an all-or-nothing affair.

WEIGHING COSTS

The upshot of all this is that sometimes, you should speak your mind even as this invites social costs—for your own sake. Remember that ultimately, social status is not what makes life worth living. Upon reflection this will seem right to most of us. Imagine a life lacking all virtue and genuine achievement, but nonetheless replete with lots of social status. Is this a life that on reflection we have reason to endorse or be proud of? Similarly, if Aristotle and Nietzsche are right, then pleasure can't be the ultimate goal of life either. Now of course, social status and pleasure are often very helpful for us to flourish in life: typically, we can't achieve good things if we're constantly in pain or if nobody takes us seriously. But in the end, it's important to remember that these goals are subordinate to the goal of living a good life, whatever that may be.

Now, Aristotle gives us a particular conception of the good life—namely, one where we develop and exercise our rational capacities well. But if Shiffrin is right, then doing this requires us to express our thoughts and ideas outwardly and to receive feedback from others. Sometimes, doing so conflicts with the goals of social status and pleasure. In these cases, we must weigh the costs and the benefits—keeping in mind what the ultimate goal is. If we fully sacrifice our rational capacities at the altar of social status and pleasure, we end up living bad lives. This is not to say we should always speak our minds, regardless of the costs. In some cases, the costs can be high enough that they defeat the very goal of trying to develop our rational capacities. Thus, imagine a case (all too common in history) where speaking your mind will invite execution by the authorities. You can't exercise your rational capacities if you're dead. And so, keeping your mouth shut in such a case may well be the thing to do, even with regards to promoting the goal that Aristotle sets out for a good human life.

Aristotle's teacher's teacher, Socrates, disputed even this. Though he left no extant writings, we get a general picture of what Socrates was like from his pupil, Plato. The picture is one of a "gadfly," who went around questioning the most basic assumptions of Athenians at the time. Socrates would put to test their views about piety, justice, love, courage, and more. Often, he would point out that what many Athenians took for granted on these topics did not hold up under philosophical scrutiny. Plato's early dialogues featuring Socrates typically end in *aporia*, or a state of impasse. No positive account or theory of a concept is offered; the dialogue is rather meant to show simply that the basic assumptions taken as given regarding the concept are untenable.

In part because he went around challenging assumptions in this way, Socrates was put to death by an Athenian jury. In other words, Socrates was executed for speaking his mind. Yet he famously declared, as his trial was taking place, that being put to death in this way was preferable to a life of intellectual obedience. If those were his only options, he'd choose death gladly, and do it all over again. He says, in the *Apology*:

> as long as I draw breath and am able, I shall not cease to practice philosophy, to exhort you and in my usual way to point out to any one of you whom I happen to meet: 'Good sir, you are an Athenian, a citizen of the greatest city with the greatest reputation for both wisdom and power; are you not ashamed of your eagerness to possess as much wealth, reputation and honors as possible, while you do not care for nor give thought to wisdom or truth, or the best possible state of your soul?'[12]

Wealth and reputation cannot be the ultimate goods, for Socrates. He will continue to question people who lead their lives as if these things are to be pursued at the expense of wisdom or truth. "Wealth," he says, "does not bring about excellence, but excellence makes wealth and everything else good for men, both individually and collectively."[13] Sacrificing our rational capacities for the sake of wealth, then, is counterproductive in Socrates's view; it is not the way to live a good life.

Rather, the pursuit of wealth (and therefore pleasure and social status, which wealth is a means to achieving) must be properly subordinated to the pursuit of excellence—which can only be attained by speaking our minds. "I have deliberately not led a quiet life,"[14] he says, as he is explaining why he did not primarily pursue status, wealth, or political power. Pursuing these things, according to him, within the context that he lived in, would have meant sacrificing either his honesty or his disposition to express his thoughts. These are not a price worth paying if the goal is to live a good life. Socrates says, "the greatest good for a man [is] to discuss virtue every day and those other things about which you hear me conversing and testing myself and others, for the unexamined life is not worth living."[15] What thus comes out in the *Apology* is a view on which not only are wealth, prestige, and status unworthy goals for which to sacrifice one's integrity, but even death itself is preferable to the option of never speaking your mind about the important issues of human life.

Now, we need not follow Socrates all the way to death here— if speaking your mind means death, then perhaps don't speak your mind. But we should remember that if pleasure and status are not the ultimate goods in life, and if the proper development and exercise of our rational capacities, on the other hand, is the (or at least *an*) ultimate good, then sacrificing the latter for the former is perverse. The sacrifice should only be performed if the detriments to our prospects for status or pleasure are expected to be *so great* that speaking our minds in that particular instance will undermine our ability to develop our rational agency in the long run. For example, if speaking your mind on issue X means losing your job, and if losing your job means a life of constant anxiety or menial drudgery, with little scope for rational excellence, then you should not speak your mind on X right then and there—at least as far as *your* living a good life is concerned. Keep the powder dry.

REASON IS ESSENTIALLY SOCIAL

Now, to understand what it is to reason well, we need to inquire into the nature of reason. What is it? What is reason's function? Why do humans reason?

The traditional picture in philosophy has been that reason helps us get to the truth on complex matters. Direct perception can tell us about our surrounding world. For example, it allows us to see that there is a tree in the yard. Direct perception can only go so far though. When we need to figure out things that we can't directly see or feel or smell, we use our faculty of reason to conduct an inference, by which we come to the truth on matters that are not directly perceptible. Reason allows us to draw new conclusions based on information we already have. For example, we might look at the streets, see that they are wet, and infer that it has been raining. Similarly, we can use reasoning to figure out more complex matters: about the stock market, or science, or the optimal design of an airplane. We can call this the "intellectualist" view of reason.

Recent work in psychology undermines the intellectualist view. In their book *The Enigma of Reason*, cognitive scientists Hugo Mercier and Dan Sperber argue for an interactionist picture of reason. According to this picture, the function of reason is *not* to help individuals arrive at the truth by themselves; rather its function is *essentially social*. Reason is but one module of inference among many. Our perceptual and other bodily faculties are making inferences all the time. Facial recognition, for example, involves inference: the inputs are visual stimuli and the output is a conclusion about who the person is. Even ants make inferences when they figure out how to get back to the colony after finding food. Inferences are everywhere in our physical and psychological makeup, as well as those of creatures like ants, slugs, and mosquitos. What is special about reason is not that it allows for inference, but rather that it allows us to *justify* what we believe and how we act to others. We use reasoning to make a special kind of inference: inference about reasons, which are considerations that we can use to justify ourselves to others. We also employ this faculty to evaluate the reasons of others. For instance: "Do they have a good reason to be late?"

Reasoning, say Mercier and Sperber, is an essentially social activity. If they are right, then speaking our minds is essential to the proper development and exercise of our rational capacities. If we're meant to reason with others, then we can't reason well without sharing our thoughts. We simply can't reason well by ourselves.

Mercier and Sperber offer several compelling arguments, drawing from a vast empirical literature. One core idea is that the interactionist model can explain a variety of experimental results which demonstrate the often *post hoc* way in which people come up with reasons. In other words, within the setups of a variety of experiments conducted over the years, the reasons people gave to experimenters could not have been the reasons for which they believed or acted as they did.

For example, in one study, participants were greeted by a friendly administrator who led them into a room to fill out a questionnaire. Subjects were told that they were participating in a study on games. The real experiment was to see how they would react to a situation where someone appears to need help. A while later, the administrator sounds like she climbs on a chair and there is a loud crash. She yells in pain, and cries out for someone to help her get an object off her leg. When the participants were by themselves in the room, most (70%) went out to help.

However, in a separate design, there were two people in the room. The other person was an actor who pretended to be a participant in the study as well. This person shrugged off the lady's call for help and looked unconcerned about what was happening. Strikingly, in this design, only 7% of the participants went out to try and help. But importantly, when later they were asked why they did not try to help, most insisted that the presence of the other unperturbed person had no effect on their decisions.[16] Of course, this can't be right.

Now why would people insist that the other person had no effect on their decision? Naturally admitting this would make them *look bad*. If reason's main task is to act as a lawyer for us, as Mercier and Sperber argue, this result is not surprising. But if the reasons we give are those for which we genuinely act, then the experimental results are deeply puzzling. Clearly, the participants in the second setup do not intervene due to the presence of the nonchalant confederate—so why don't they say so? Are they simply lying?

In another striking study, an experimenter approaches people on the street with a clipboard. He asks them about their positions on a variety of moral and political issues. He then asks people to justify their positions. Unbeknownst to them, however, some of the statements they assented to have been flipped so that they now say the exact opposite. Yet more than half the participants don't even notice this. In fact, they go on to state the reasons why they accept this contradictory conclusion![17] Many studies with this kind of structure have been conducted and yield similar results. Mercier and Sperber thus conclude that humans are "rationalization machines."[18]

Another piece of evidence Mercier and Sperber use to defend the interactionist model is the notorious "confirmation" or "myside" bias that reason has.[19] Our reasoning often looks for considerations that support our antecedently held beliefs. Yet, this makes it *harder* for us to come to accurate beliefs by ourselves. If that were the goal of reasoning, then it should not have a myside bias—rather it should pay close attention to disconfirming evidence as well. We should thus reject the view that the function of reasoning is to help individuals come to accurate beliefs.

Mercier and Sperber offer a helpful analogy. Consider male elk, who have enormous antlers. Now, these antlers are heavy and make it harder to evade predators. But imagine noting these two things and claiming that the function of the antlers is to make it easy for elk to avoid predators! That would be preposterous. Instead, we should look for other functions—in the case of elk, the antlers are plausibly a result of sexual selection. Their function is to attract females, not evade predators. Analogously, the function of reason is not to help individuals arrive at the truth, whatever it may be. Rather, its function is to act as a lawyer for us.

In general, the picture that emerges from decades of psychological research is that reasoning is *lazy* and *biased*. Now, this might sound depressing. If reasoning is hopelessly lazy and biased what's the point? Perhaps we should just resign ourselves. Moreover, if reasoning inevitably has these flaws, why bother trying to cultivate it?

Another option here is to dig in our heels. We might just deny that reasoning is lazy and biased. Or we might deny that it is so for *us*, or for smart, well-educated people in general. The evidence against this is quite strong—it's simply not true that smarter people are less biased. In fact, there are good reasons to suspect the opposite. For example, people with greater political sophistication and knowledge show greater levels of confirmation bias.[20] And while bias is pervasive in human reasoning, most people don't think they're biased— *other* people are biased, but not *me*, we humans tend to think. This is known as the "bias blind spot" in psychology. Greater cognitive sophistication does not mitigate this blind spot; in fact, recent studies suggest the bias blind spot may even be exacerbated by cognitive sophistication.[21]

The third option is to *embrace* the social role of reason. Mercier and Sperber suggest that the laziness and myside bias are features rather than bugs here. Reason helps us *together* to reach truths about various issues, via back and forth. And the laziness and myside bias help the division of cognitive labor to take place between participants. I'll defend X, you defend Y, and we, along with those observing us, can see what wins out. Importantly, for this to work, we must be good at assessing other people's reasons, even if we are not good at assessing our own. In fact, this turns out to be the case—we are much better at evaluating an argument we produce if we are told that it originated from someone else.[22] Our reasoning is thus *selectively lazy*: we're easy on ourselves but hard on others.

Mercier and Sperber explain:

> If we take an interactionist perspective, the traits of argument production typically seen as flaws become elegant ways to divide cognitive labor. The most difficult task, finding good reasons, is made easier by the myside bias and by sensible laziness. The myside bias makes reasoners focus on just one side of the issue rather than having to figure out on their own how to adopt everyone's perspective. Laziness lets reason stop looking for better reasons when it has found an acceptable one. The interlocutor, if not convinced, will look for a counterargument, helping the speaker produce more pointed reasons. By using bias and laziness to its advantage, the exchange of reasons offers an elegant, cost-effective way to solve a disagreement.[23]

Now, our legal system, though far predating this research in its origins, embraces these points and runs with them. Each lawyer's job is explicitly to defend their client—*not* to directly promote truth or justice. Rather, truth and justice are meant to *emerge* via court proceedings, given how the rules and incentives are set up. The institution of juries also reflects an appreciation of the limitations of sole reasoners. While sole reasoners may be hopelessly biased, juries can track the truth much more reliably, especially if they are made up of diverse individuals.[24] The hope is that each juror will check the reasoning of the others, and the truth will emerge through a process of deliberation. And given that we are better able to assess the reasoning of *others* as opposed to our own, it is the jury, not the lawyers making the case, who decide upon the verdict.

UPSHOTS FOR INDIVIDUALS AND INSTITUTIONS

If Mercier and Sperber are right, then we should think of our epistemic lives much more on the model of a courtroom than of solitary thinkers trying to arrive at the truth. Reasoning is biased but that doesn't mean we can't be good reasoners. Lawyers are explicitly meant to be biased, and yet some lawyers are better than others. Becoming a good reasoner might be in some ways like becoming a good lawyer. Perhaps, to reason well is to function as a good interlocutor in some conversation, whether it be written or verbal. And being a good interlocutor in this way, of course, is not possible without speaking your mind.

This also means that to reason well, we must find good interlocutors. That is, we must find people who we are able to have productive conversations with, who challenge our assumptions as we challenge theirs. Good interlocutors provide valuable feedback, and through a process of open back and forth, some truth or insight may be arrived at. Reasoning then, is more like tennis and less like mountain climbing. You can, in principle, climb a mountain alone, but you can't play tennis alone. For someone to exercise her tennis playing abilities and improve them, she must find others to play with—preferably, others with similar levels of skill.

What this might also mean is that we cannot reason well if we surround ourselves with others who think exactly like us. And this is borne out in social scientific research. Groups of like-minded individuals often reason very poorly, especially if they have affective ties to one another, no matter how smart or educated they are.[25] In this vein, Bertrand Russell advised, "Find more pleasure in intelligent dissent than in passive agreement, for, if you value intelligence as you should, the former implies a deeper agreement than the latter."[26] Of course, this is not to say that we must constantly engage with those who think diametrically opposite things on every single matter—this might be bad for a variety of reasons. Presumably, there is some golden mean to be achieved.

The psychological evidence marshaled above also supports a view I defended in earlier chapters—namely, that our institutions of knowledge production should be maximally tolerant of dissent if they are to work well. From an individual ethics perspective, this means doing what one can to allow dissenters to flourish, as well as producing heterodox research ourselves insofar as we are in a position to do so, despite social costs. Adding to the conversation by offering a new perspective or argument is vastly more valuable than piling on with reasons on one side of a debate. Now, as flagged earlier in the book, fields like physics or chemistry, or the subfield within philosophy called metaethics, presumably don't raise worries in this regard. But such worries might well apply to fields or areas of inquiry where there exists strong enough social pressure not to offer certain arguments or pursue research that undermines particular conclusions.

In general, if reasoning is an essentially social activity, then the social conditions and incentives must be right in order for us to reason well. And if these conditions are not right with respect to inquiry within a particular domain, then our collective epistemic condition with regards to that domain is almost certainly impoverished or warped in some way. As individuals, we thus might have little reason to trust the outputs of our institutions of (ostensible) knowledge production with regards to such domains.

CONCLUSION

If reasoning is an essentially social activity, as Mercier and Sperber claim, we cannot reason well without speaking our minds. Insofar as the ancient Greek philosophers were right that the excellent use of our rational capacities is what makes human life go well, then this idea has a very important upshot: speaking your mind is essential to cultivating your rational capacities as a human being, and hence, living well.

If we censor ourselves so as to never raise doubts, contribute evidence, or ask a question when doing so rubs up against social pressure, we become stunted and imprisoned as rational beings. Perhaps we might achieve expertise in a narrow, non-politicized subfield, but we cannot become good, well-rounded thinkers in this way. Some may well be contented to live like this. They might not even feel the social pressure if they're satisfied to live within its confines at all times. But this is no way to flourish as a human being.

Five

> As there are persons in the world of so mean and abject a spirit, that they rather choose to owe their subsistence to the charity of others, than by industry to acquire some property of their own; so there are many more who may be called mere beggars with regard to their opinions. Through laziness and indifference about the truth, they leave to others the drudgery of digging for this commodity; they can have enough at second hand to serve their occasions. Their concern is not to know what is true, but what is said and thought on such subjects; and their understanding, like their clothes, is cut according to the fashion.
>
> —Thomas Reid, *Essays on the Powers of the Human Mind*

This chapter claims that the *independent* exercise of our distinctive human capacities—whatever they may turn out to be—is a necessary element of a great life. The picture defended here subsumes the idea of the previous chapter. If reasoning is the distinctive human capacity, then the excellent use of reason must manifest independence: in other words, we must think for ourselves. On the other hand, this chapter does not take for granted the Aristotelian notion that reason is the only distinctive feature of humans; here, we can leave open what the distinctive features are. Whatever they are, though, a good human life manifests the independent exercise of them.

I want to suggest that an individual can only live a great life if she develops her own ideas and perspectives rather than simply conforming to and adopting, as if by osmosis, the values and assumptions of her milieu. Furthermore, to develop this independence, it is necessary to cultivate a disposition to speak our minds—or express ourselves more broadly, through ways of life, art, etc.

Now this is not to say that independence of this sort is a *sufficient* condition for a great life; it's just a necessary condition. For instance, we can be met with external misfortune, which might stop us from actualizing a great life. Imagine a writer or entrepreneur with great potential who dies in a car accident before her ideas can come into fruition. It's natural to say that though she had the potential to lead a great life, the actual misfortune she suffered prevented her from achieving a great life.

Furthermore, the independence discussed here doesn't simply amount to contrarianism. A contrarian is someone who disagrees just for the sake of disagreeing. Say the Earth is round, and he will say it is flat. Say it is flat, and he will say it is round. While this person *looks* like he is independent, in a deeper sense, he is not. The independence is superficial. For, he lets the world dictate his opinion: if the world points north, he will point south; if it points east, he will point west. Others blow with the wind, and he blows in the opposite direction. The wind still determines his trajectory completely. Thus, in a way, he is still defined by his milieu—he does not live in independence from it.

What is meant by a 'great' life? A great life is one that, as a whole, we have reason to take pride in. It is also a proper object of admiration and respect from others. Perhaps it also has a kind of aesthetic quality—so that we may appreciate a great life like we appreciate a great painting or literary masterpiece. Now what is the *argument* for why independence is necessary for a great life? I suspect the best one can do here is to point at a conformist life and hope the reader finds it wanting.

Bison and wildebeest move in herds; likewise, schooling fish like sardines also exhibit similar behavior. There's usually no leader of the herd, but each herd animal takes its cues from others and the whole group moves in unison. Each animal will have no real sense of why the herd is moving where it is. An individual sardine might not perceive the predator the school is trying to escape from—it simply feels comfortable when moving in the same direction as the others, and that's why it does what it does. Even if there was no predator, it would move with the school; and if the school changes its direction for no real reason at all, so be it—the sardine will move with them nonetheless. Within the non-human animal kingdom, we can contrast this with the behavior of leopards or tigers. Even though these creatures act mostly by instinct, they still act in a kind of autonomous, purposeful manner.

Now consider a person who conducts his mental life as wildebeest or sardines conduct their physical lives. He just moves with the popular opinion of the time—in particular that of his milieu. He looks to social media influencers, peers, and so on, to determine what opinion is in fashion at the moment. His milieu often moves like a herd. The thing to think now is X, the thing to get outraged about today is Y; tomorrow it might be Z that one must express outrage about. Such an individual may not conceive of himself as a copycat (we often try to have flattering opinions about ourselves) but as the milieu moves, so does he. There's little if anything by way of "my social group thinks X, but is X really true?" "Does

X conflict with some other belief or ideal the group holds?" "Of all the things going on in the world, is Y the thing deserving our attention the most?" "Do the basic values taken for granted by my social group make sense?" He rarely entertains such questions, and definitely never voices them—for, doing the latter might invite social cost. He thinks and says whatever he feels like gets the most praise and other positive feedback from his network.

Try to picture a person like this. Is this person living a great life? It's almost like someone designed an artificial intelligence that could pass the Turing Test and optimized it for absorbing the zeitgeist, doing and saying what the zeitgeist rewards so as to gain social status. The life of such a mental herd-animal cannot be great in the way described earlier. It might contain pleasure and status—but if it doesn't contain independence, it doesn't seem worthy of appreciation and admiration in a certain way.

This strand of thinking runs through both John Stuart Mill and Friedrich Nietzsche—two great philosophers who were climbing a mountain from different sides, so to speak. Both thought that the great life must exhibit independence. A life of mental conformity is ipso facto not great. Aside from resisting conformity so as to help society (though, such altruistic concerns are more prevalent in Mill than Nietzsche), we should also resist it for our own sakes, insofar as we want to lead great lives.

While this chapter will focus on Mill and Nietzsche, many great philosophers throughout history have echoed this idea in some form or another. Consider for example, Immanuel Kant. Kant doesn't have much in common with Mill or Nietzsche. Utilitarianism, an idea Mill defended, is often taken to be the main rival for Kantian ethics. And Nietzsche reserved some of his harshest criticisms for Kant's ideas. Yet here is Kant, in an essay he wrote about the Enlightenment:

> Have courage to make use of your own understanding! is thus the motto of enlightenment. It is because of laziness and cowardice that so great a part of humankind, after nature has long since emancipated them from other people's direction . . . nevertheless gladly remains minors for life . . . It is so comfortable to be a minor! . . . That by far the greatest part of humankind . . . should hold the step toward majority to be not only troublesome but also highly dangerous will soon be seen to by those guardians who have kindly taken it upon themselves to supervise them; after they have made their domesticated animals dumb and carefully prevented these placid creatures from daring to take a single step without the walking cart in which they have confined them.[1]

An exhortation towards the independent use of our thinking is thus a recurring pattern among great historical philosophers who otherwise disagreed on many fundamental issues.

Importantly for our purposes, speaking your mind is essential to both developing independence and constitutive of it. An independence worth cultivating cannot be achieved by keeping all your thoughts to yourself. For, if reasoning is a social activity, then we cannot reason well unless we share our nascent thoughts with interlocutors. Furthermore, thoughts are often not well formed unless they are expressed in some way—written down, verbalized, and so on. It is plausible that whatever other distinctive human capacities we might have are essentially social in this way as well. Indeed, it's a platitude that humans are social animals. Moreover, a person who refuses to express the slightest dissent given the faintest whiff of social pressure cannot be said to manifest independence in any real sense. Independence in part involves a willingness to resist social pressure, though not necessarily all the way to execution, like Socrates. It is thus a character trait that has an outward manifestation.

If speaking your mind is necessary for cultivating and manifesting independence, and if the latter is a necessary feature of the great life, then in order to lead a great life, it is necessary for us to speak our minds. In what follows, my aim is to draw on several different threads in Mill and Nietzsche to paint a picture of the kind of independence that they saw as worthwhile in and of itself. I will also examine some of the dangers and pitfalls these authors warn about vis-à-vis cultivating independence and tie their discussion to issues and trends that are alive today.

INDEPENDENCE AS CONSTITUTIVE OF A GREAT LIFE

Mill famously thought that an extensive sphere of liberty should be afforded to each individual; he is thus a sort of patron saint of classical liberalism. According to Mill, the state should not interfere with people when they're doing things that concern only themselves in a certain sense. Thus, he opposed paternalistic laws—that is, laws meant to be for the citizen's own good. Examples of such laws might include prohibitions against drinking or smoking marijuana.

One of Mill's reasons for opposing paternalism is that there are no one-size-fits-all rules as to what might bring people happiness or what might help them flourish. Drinking alcohol may be a bad idea for some (e.g. those susceptible to addiction or those who have certain health problems) but not for others.

Moreover, people find joy, meaning, excitement in different things. And so there ought to be a variety of "experiments in living" so that each individual can determine what kind of life would be best for them. To each his own.

Another reason we might want to promote individuality is that free thinking allows people to make new discoveries in all kinds of ways. We need people to question whether particular norms of society are in fact healthy and just, and if not, show new ways forward. The great discoveries and inventions of social and natural science are also only possible if individuals are able to speak their minds and contest the assumptions and models of the day.[2] So far so good. But these are all instrumental reasons for pursuing and promoting independence. Independence is claimed to be good because it lets people find out for themselves what kind of life is most satisfying to them, and it allows some people to make discoveries that benefit others. Many readers will find this true and perhaps somewhat banal. This is also the idea that modern commentators and political philosophers tend to emphasize from Mill.[3]

But the much more interesting claim, one that Mill is at pains to stress, is that independence is not only valuable because it allows us to pursue other goods, but rather that it is extremely valuable in itself. In fact, he explicitly laments that he needs to show why independence, as developed by some, is going to be instrumentally valuable for others, so as to convince the majority of his readers that independence is valuable in some way or another. And early on in Chapter 3 of On Liberty, he says: "the evil is, that individual spontaneity is hardly recognized by the common modes of thinking, as having any intrinsic worth, or deserving any regard on its own account."[4] Regrettably, for Mill, "Originality is the one thing which unoriginal minds cannot feel the use of."[5]

Why is individuality valuable in itself? We get something like an argument in Chapter 3. It is a teleological argument in the vein of Aristotle. If we reflect on human nature, Mill thinks, we will realize that a human being cannot genuinely flourish if it merely *copies*—it must also *create*. Some objects and creatures do flourish by merely copying. To use a previous example, consider the sardine. Given the kind of thing that a sardine is—namely, a schooling fish—it thrives when it follows the school. A sardine that goes its own way will get stressed, fail to find food, and get eaten quickly—and moreover, its good consists largely in avoiding these things. But human beings are not like sardines. We achieve excellence only if we develop and exercise our own independent thoughts, perspectives, and ways of living. Thus, Mill says:

> Human nature is not a machine to be built after a model, and set to do exactly the work prescribed for it, but a tree, which requires to grow and develop itself on all sides, according to the tendency of the inward forces that make it a living thing . . . One whose desires and impulses are not his own, has no character, no more than a steam-engine has character.[6]

He continues, in what is one of the most eloquent passages within *On Liberty*: "It is not by wearing down into uniformity all that is individual in themselves, but by cultivating it and calling it forth, within the limits imposed by the rights and interests of others, that human beings become a noble and beautiful object of contemplation."[7]

For Nietzsche as well, independence is a necessary component of a great life. A great individual, according to him, is one who, among other things, *creates his own values*.[8] Only such an individual can live a noble life, one that has a certain *aesthetic* value of the sort we appreciate in a great work of literature.[9] To create one's own values involves refusing to take those of the surrounding culture for granted. In his own context, these were what he called the "Christian" values (though I suspect he would consider today's values much more Christian). Even as the European intelligentsia were secularizing at the time, Nietzsche thought that the morality of the time was still a deeply Christian one.

The philosopher in particular (and he often stressed that he didn't mean philosophy professors) would challenge the moral values of his time and forge a new path forward. He says:

> More and more it seems to me that the philosopher, being *of necessity* a man of tomorrow and the day after tomorrow, has always found himself, and *had* to find himself, in contradiction to his today: his enemy was ever the ideal of today. So far all these extraordinary furtherers of man whom one calls philosophers, though they themselves have rarely felt like friends of wisdom but rather like disagreeable fools and dangerous question marks, have found their task, their hard, unwanted, inescapable task, but eventually also the greatness of their task, in being the bad conscience of their time. By applying the knife vivisectionally to the chest of the very *virtues of their time*, they betrayed what was their own secret: to know of a new greatness of man, of a new untrodden way to his enhancement.[10]

A philosopher thus displays a deep kind of independence. It's not merely independence in terms of style of clothing, or food choice, or taste in music: these things are easy to come by. Rather, the independence the philosopher displays is *evaluative* independence—he is willing and able to challenge the most basic evaluative assumptions that his milieu takes for granted. Being a philosopher in this way must come with being misunderstood or considered dangerous and evil, or both.[11] Hence, Nietzsche expected that he too would be misunderstood and thus be "born posthumously."[12] But though his task is thus perilous, the philosopher rejoices in it. He embraces and cultivates his independence, without succumbing to the pressure to conform. Nietzsche encourages those who have the capacity to become philosophers in this sense to throw caution to the wind and plunge into war—war against the comfortable moral assumptions of their age. He says:

> For believe me: the secret for harvesting from existence the greatest fruitfulness and the greatest enjoyment is—to live dangerously! Build your cities on the slopes of Vesuvius! Send your ships into uncharted seas. Live at war with your peers and yourselves! Be robbers and conquerors as long as you cannot be rulers and possessors, you seekers of knowledge![13]

Of course, he is not here talking about physical robbery or danger. Rather, the danger goes deeper than that—it is a spiritual danger. Reevaluating the values that you grow up with, that you are constantly surrounded by, that you are told it's evil to challenge or even critically examine and question, is a dangerous task. It can really feel like going into an uncharted sea, where nobody has sailed before. What storms might lie ahead?

Non-philosophers can be great too, for Nietzsche. Beethoven, for instance, is someone he often mentions as a paradigm case of a great individual. But part of Beethoven's greatness lies in his innovation; we consider him to be a great composer because of where music was at the time and what had come before. Someone who composed similar symphonies today would presumably not be considered great, and rightly so. In this way, greatness essentially involves standing out, relative to the culture and historical context of one's time—though of course merely standing out is not sufficient.[14]

Because it involves standing out and striving, a great life, for Nietzsche, is emphatically not a comfortable life. A great life must in some way involve suffering: to strive is to suffer. This suffering might for instance include periods of self-doubt or frustration or a feeling of alienation from others. People who cultivate independence at a high level and refuse to follow the herd in their assumptions are bound to feel lonely and somewhat alienated.[15] All this is perhaps a foreign way of looking at life from the 21st century perspective, but for Nietzsche, a great individual does not always seek to avoid suffering— sometimes he even seeks it out!

Moreover, Nietzsche is not simply thinking that some individuals must take on suffering so that they can serve others, or that the suffering has some material payoff (pleasure or wealth or status in the long run). For him, this would be a rather superficial and materialistic way of thinking about it. Instead, at least on one way of reading Nietzsche, the idea is that the interestingly and importantly independent life, which is in and of itself of great value, cannot be one of comfort. It takes a lot of striving and struggle to achieve great things—and the striving itself, the overcoming, is valuable.[16]

Nietzsche acknowledges that a lot of people will be puzzled at this way of seeing things. "Common natures," he says, "consider all noble, magnanimous feelings inexpedient and therefore first of all incredible . . . When they are irresistibly persuaded of the absence of selfish intentions and gains, they see the noble person as a kind of fool."[17] According to Nietzsche, most people will have difficulty seeing the merit of the kind of independence he recommends. They might ask: what is to be gained? What's in it for me? Similarly, Nietzsche also thinks, the "noble" person will have a hard time understanding the "common"—why would they not relish the independence he relishes? "For the most part," writes Nietzsche, the noble type "assumes that its own passion is present but kept concealed in all men, and this belief even becomes an ardent and eloquent faith."[18]

As emphasized earlier, independence must be something more than simple contrarianism if it is to be valuable. If what Nietzsche is recommending is simply being different for the sake of being different, then this doesn't seem like a very noble ideal. Such a person would still be allowing herself to be defined by the crowd. However, one way to understand what Nietzsche is getting at here is that a great individual does not have that same need to conform to the values and assumptions of her milieu. Many people do have this need; but only (a subset of) the few who don't, are for Nietzsche, capable of living great lives. "One must shed the bad taste of wanting to agree with the many," he says.[19] When someone sheds this bad taste, then she can be free to decide for herself whether the values her peers reflexively adopt and profess are actually worthwhile. Such a person might be able to lead an interestingly and importantly unique life.

INDEPENDENCE AS THE PRIVILEGE OF THE FEW

As the above discussion suggests, Nietzsche thinks that most people, unfortunately, cannot develop into independent thinkers. Most people are bound to follow the comfortable path and, moreover, will be puzzled as to why anyone would want not to. In what he considered to be his best work, *Thus Spoke Zarathustra*, Nietzsche's mouthpiece, Zarathustra, a kind of sage who emerges from a period of solitude and reflection, initially seeks to impart his teachings to the whole of humanity. "Behold," declares Zarathustra, "I am weary of my wisdom, like a bee that has gathered too much honey; I need hands outstretched to receive it."[20] But soon after he actually meets and tries to talk with the people in the marketplace, where he goes first, he becomes disillusioned. They greet him either with laughter or puzzlement. Zarathustra then decides only to speak to fellow travelers. "An insight has come to me," he says, "let Zarathustra speak not to the people but to companions . . . To lure many away from the herd, for that I have come." He continues a bit later, "Behold the good and the just! Whom do they hate most? The man who breaks their tables of values, the breaker, the lawbreaker; yet he is the creator."[21]

Thus, many people—especially those who pride themselves on being morally upstanding and righteous—will despise those who challenge their values and seek to persecute them. In this way, the "good and the just" are a prime obstacle to the progress of mankind.[22] And the majority will simply either endorse the herd morality or will not be courageous enough to think for themselves. It's all a hopeless task, Nietzsche comes to think. But he then changes strategy—instead of resigning completely, he decides to write for and speak to the few who are able to break away.

Elsewhere, Nietzsche puts it more bluntly. For example, in *Beyond Good and Evil*, he says, "Independence is for the very few; it is a privilege of the strong."[23] And in the *Gay Science*, he laments:

> I do not want to believe it although it is palpable: *the great majority of people lacks an intellectual conscience.* Indeed, it has

often seemed to me as if anyone calling for an intellectual conscience were as lonely in the most densely populated cities as if he were in a desert . . . I mean: *the great majority of people* does not consider it contemptible to believe this or that and to live accordingly, without first having given themselves an account of the final and most certain reasons pro and con, and without even troubling themselves about such reasons afterward.[24]

Thus, most people will believe and say what is fashionable or comfortable to believe and say, without genuinely caring about whether it is justified. Many people's moral and social commitments will thus be more or less determined by the ethos and incentives within their milieu—but of course these are not proper *reasons* to believe things. The fact that everyone around you thinks justice demands X is no reason to believe that justice demands X. Rather, the intellectually honest person— one with a conscience—will inquire for *herself* whether justice really demands X. Her beliefs about morality and justice will not be matters of *fashion* for her; rather she will take such matters seriously. What are the reasons for thinking justice demands X? What about the following problem? Is this idea of justice compatible with this other commitment people around me seem to have? And so on.

Mill also thought that individuality was rare in his time. In the case of most people, Mill said, "it does not occur to them to have any inclination, except for what is customary. Thus the mind itself is bowed to the yoke."[25] Though, in contrast with Nietzsche, Mill is somewhat more interested in the kinds of social and political conditions that allow great minds to flourish. And he is far more sanguine about the prospects for society-wide promotion of independence and individuality.[26] He is thus at pains to advocate for social norms and laws that allow individuals as much latitude as possible—in their speech, lifestyle, and behavior—so long as it is consistent with the same latitude for others.

Such a society is desirable for Mill in part because it promotes the development of exceptional individuals. Because he thinks "persons of genius" are rarely able to fit themselves into the particular ways of living that a rigid society can allow for, it is important to have norms that allow individuals to pursue their own life plans as much as possible.[27]

EDUCATION AS SOLUTION?

In this vein, it is worth inquiring further into what conditions promote the flourishing of individuals, allowing them to develop independence of thought and value. One common refrain here is that this is the function of education. Ideally, through education, people can learn to think critically, for themselves, and not take society's values and assumptions for granted. Indeed, this is part of the justification for the vast and expensive systems of modern education.

Mill worried about whether education can be a *deus ex machina* in this way. Just because the overt aim of something is X, we cannot conclude that it actually succeeds in achieving X. If it is not carefully structured, education might actually *breed conformity* rather than alleviating it. As mentioned in earlier chapters, the key for Mill is creating an ethos of open discussion about all matters—even those we consider most foundational or sacred. Only then can we be justified in believing as we do. However, he laments, that in his time:

Ninety-nine in a hundred of what are called educated men are in this condition; even of those who can argue fluently for their opinions. Their conclusion may be true, but it might be false for anything they know: they have never thrown themselves into the mental position of those who think differently from them, and considered what such persons may have to say; and consequently they do not, in any proper sense of the word, know the doctrine they themselves profess.[28]

Thus, educational institutions can fail in their mission of promoting truth and cultivating independence if they only allow one side of an issue to be heard, and if they do not allow for a robust exchange of ideas across diverse viewpoints. Mill's is not an *anti-intellectual* stance; rather, it reflects a deep respect for intellectual rigor. But the mere granting of degrees is not sufficient for the cultivation of such rigor; it is all too important for the institutions of higher learning to be structured the right way.

To the extent that education on a particular moral or political issue cultivates in students the disposition to think there is only one reasonable view on the matter, and to demonize those holding other perspectives, it can be counterproductive. Nietzsche puts the point thus: "The surest way to corrupt a youth is to instruct him to hold in higher esteem those who think alike than those who think differently."[29] One of his worries was that the German university system of his time, far from allowing individuals to challenge social values and assumptions, rather produced conformity on these matters. *Philosophers*, in his sense, find it hard to flourish within the university.[30] Independence of thought, then, is far from a guaranteed outcome of formal education, however noble its stated aims.

Elsewhere, Nietzsche worries that the pressure for scholars to specialize heavily can undermine the potential for creativity and independence. In a colorful passage in *Zarathustra*, he likens scholars to "flour bags," "mills," and "frogs," among other things, who "pursue knowledge as if it were nut-cracking." He then says he would rather sleep on "ox hides than on their decorums and respectabilities."[31] We might worry here about whether Nietzsche adequately appreciates the need for cognitive division of labor in producing knowledge. Perhaps he is too critical of specialization. Be that as it may, he might be right that one pernicious side effect of specialization (even if it is on the whole a good thing) is that it leaves little room for people to ask the big questions and give innovative answers. For Nietzsche, the university system, as it is set up, can produce "philosophical laborers" but discourages the development of philosophers.[32]

POLITICS AND CONFORMITY

Another danger for developing independence is attention to and consumption of politics. Political parties and platforms, by their very design, encourage conformity and stifle independence, as Nietzsche sees it. As noted earlier in this book, parties have an incentive to create a strong coalition. Thus, parties encourage the adoption of a whole package of views, the connections among which may be simply accidents of history. For instance, a good member of either political tribe today, in the United States, has prescribed and predictable views on immigration, minimum wage, crime and policing, abortion, environmental policy—even if the reasons that would justify particular positions on these issues are quite different from one to the other. Political tribes are not hospitable locations for independent thinkers. "Whoever thinks much is not suitable as a party member;" Nietzsche says, "he soon thinks himself right through the party."[33]

Independent thinkers will thus try to avoid politics, inso-far as they can.[34] Politics is shallow, and its alliances are ever-shifting. Parties change their platforms when it is conve-nient for maximizing votes and expect their ranks to follow without question. Politics is also typically not the place to challenge popular convictions. The Nietzschean philosopher will thus eschew day-to-day politics and focus his attention instead on fundamental questions that nobody dares to ask. Hence, he says:

> One must be skilled in living on mountains—seeing the wretched ephemeral babble of politics . . . *beneath* oneself. One must have become indifferent; one must never ask if the truth is useful or if it may prove our undoing. The pre-dilection of strength for questions for which no one today has the courage; the courage for the *forbidden.*[35]

Now, democratic politics is, after all, democratic. There is no legal compulsion for people to conform to any party line. This creates the pleasant illusion for many people that their thoughts on democratic politics are their own. They fail to recognize that many of their opinions, especially if they con-form to one party line or the other, are produced via a kind of external manipulation. The manipulation can take various forms—it may be subtle or explicit social pressure, or it may be the biased presentation of evidence within the media con-sumed by party ranks. Thus, even as democratic party poli-tics breeds conformity, it "flatters and wins the favor of all those who would like to *seem* independent and individual."[36] Party platforms then, are consumed and endorsed by people who don't think independently but *conceive of themselves* as being independent. In today's world, for example, it seems all too common to observe people presenting, in a predictable way, an opinion that lines up with what is rewarded within their social network, but nonetheless expressing it as though it were the output of their independent take on things. In this way we can observe what might be called a herd of independent thinkers.

THE FLOURISHING OF GREAT INDIVIDUALS AND "CHRISTIAN" MORALITY

Nietzsche is famous for his criticism of Christian values. For him, these values—of equality, asceticism, and pity—were life-denying. The Nietzschean ideal human being would rather embrace life-affirming values, prizing excellence, overcoming, and a certain kind of nobility. It is a tough interpretive question whether and to what extent Nietzsche thinks that great individuals can thrive despite living in a culture that embraces Christian morality.[37] However, it's safe to say that according to Nietzsche, Christian morality does not fundamentally prize the flourishing of great individuals, and is thus off the mark.

Less emphasized in this regard are Mill's views on the topic. While Nietzsche was an atheist, Mill was an overt Christian. But in a passage that might as well have been written by Nietzsche, Mill says with dismay that the Christian morality of his time prizes "Innocence rather than Nobleness," has a "horror of sensuality," makes an "idol of asceticism," and is a "doctrine of passive obedience." Like Nietzsche, Mill pays homage to ancient Greek and Roman ethics, and praises "high-mindedness, personal dignity . . . and the sense of honour."[38]

Both philosophers thus see Christian morality, interpreted in a certain way, as antithetical to the values of independence and nobility. Now, their analyses of Christianity per se may well be off the mark. Mill, given his religious beliefs, qualified his criticism by claiming that Christian morality only contains a *half-truth*, which, for him, is the most that can be achieved by any one perspective or ideology. Moreover, both Nietzsche and Mill might have been largely reacting to the *practice* of Christian values over time, as opposed to anything essential to the religion's teaching.

But what's more interesting for our purposes is that if they are right to prize the values they do, it behooves us in the 21st century to reflect on what the morality of our own age prizes and whether its values are healthy. What are the values implicit in the cultural products—books, movies, ad campaigns, magazine think pieces—of our time? Of course, there are large academic industries which purport to do just this. But it seems to me that little attention has been paid to the kind of critique Nietzsche in particular had in mind.[39] This type of critical project presents us with many low hanging fruits, ripe for the picking.

HONESTY

Nietzsche was an "immoralist" in many ways, who often seems to critique the very institution of morality, disavowing the distinctively moral virtues.[40] However, he nonetheless seems to pride one of them, often above all else—honesty. Honesty is the one virtue from which "we cannot get away," he says. It is the "only one left to us."[41] The truth about morality and about society is not always comfortable. Indeed, for Nietzsche "our highest insights" will sound either absurd or downright evil to the culture of our time.[42] Yet, the amount of truth that we can bear without flinching—that is the measure of a soul for Nietzsche.[43]

How can we develop and practice this honesty? Honesty seems to be intimately connected with independence. Someone who goes along with each popular opinion and fad seems to lack honesty in a way. He believes things not because he has reason to believe them (though he may convince himself that he does) but simply, rather, to fit in and appear upstanding. This is a kind of nonchalance about the truth—fundamentally, the truth just does not seem to matter to him. Rather, what fundamentally matters seems to be how professing certain opinions makes him look to others—in particular whether it makes him look good with respect to the public morality of his social circle. Internal comfort might matter too; he wants to believe what is comfortable. But this seems to reflect a deep sort of inauthenticity: for Nietzsche, it's a deeper dishonesty than a straightforward lie.[44] Perhaps the cherry on top of the pie here is that such a person will often deny that comfort or the desire for social status has anything to do with his stated outlook.

One thing we may wonder about is how honesty connects with speaking one's mind. Might we be internally honest without expressing dissent or asking questions? Presumably, honesty of the kind Nietzsche is referring to cannot simply amount to an internal disposition. Rather, someone who is honest seeks to voice her genuine opinions and ask questions even if they are unsettling. Of course, she may keep silent if the costs are going to be too high, but she won't balk at any social pressure whatsoever. She doesn't want to assent to something simply because it lets her fit in or makes her feel comfortable. She has a fundamental desire not to live a lie, and perhaps doesn't want her surrounding culture to live a lie either. She doesn't try to reinterpret her life so as to shoehorn it to fit within the values that she is encouraged to profess. Rather she *embraces* the values implicit in her actions. For example, she might refuse to profess an ideal like egalitarianism if her actions and life choices do not reflect that ideal—even if professing that ideal makes her feel like a good person or scores points within her social circle.

CONVICTION

Evaluative independence manifests itself in a willingness to *question*. Modern culture, on the other hand, assumes that great individuals are people of strong *conviction*. They hold certain ideals and go farther than others in defending them. Readers can verify this for themselves, by taking a cursory glance at those who are prized today as visionaries and heroes. For Nietzsche, this is not the case—greatness is not borne out of conviction. "Convictions are more dangerous enemies of truth than lies," he says.[45] The dark side of conviction is that it can blind us to contrary evidence: it can exacerbate our well-known tendency towards confirmation bias. Moreover, many people tend to take their convictions off the shelf, consuming pre-manufactured ideals that can assuage feelings of guilt or meaninglessness. In this way, convictions often come from the outside. By contrast, "great spirits," Nietzsche says, "are skeptics. Zarathustra is a skeptic. Strength, *freedom* which is born of the strength and overstrength of the spirit, proves itself by skepticism. Men of conviction are not worthy of the least consideration in fundamental questions of value and disvalue. Convictions are prisons."[46]

Often, the several convictions one is supposed to hold, in order to be considered upstanding and good, can stand in tension with one another. But a person without the disposition to be hard on himself, without a robust disposition to question, might not notice the tension at all. He might also ignore or suppress doubts raised by the questioning few. Convictions, especially if they are mandated by popular opinion, are not meant to be questioned, by design. Thus, "tolerance toward oneself permits several convictions, and they get along with each other . . . How does one compromise oneself today? If one is consistent. If one proceeds in a straight line. If one is not ambiguous enough to permit five conflicting interpretations. If one is genuine."[47] For Nietzsche, great individuals are not easy on themselves in this way—they're not tolerant towards themselves. Rather, they are hard on themselves as far as fundamental beliefs and assumptions go; they are willing to question what they (are supposed to) hold dear.

Mill echoes this idea—for him, great thinkers are not only smart, but also honest. Therefore, they will hold no ideal as sacred: nothing will be out of bounds for questioning for them. "No one can be a great thinker," says Mill, "who does not recognize that as a thinker it is his first duty to follow his intellect to whatever conclusions it may lead."[48] This is naturally easier said than done. Because our biases are imperceptible to us, we tend to assume that whatever conclusions we reach are arrived at by properly considering the balance of reasons. But perhaps one useful heuristic here is an examination of our convictions—do we hold certain ideals as sacrosanct and beyond question? If so, we might not always be following the argument wherever it leads. As massive objects warp the fabric of spacetime, convictions might warp our thinking on adjacent issues.

homogenization of culture. Because of social media in particular, the culture across the world (particularly within the West) moves as if in unison. Influencers within social media engage in social comparison with their peers and thus compete to express fashionable opinions. But their output crosses regional and national boundaries and is consumed across the world. Thus, the resident of a small village in Austria or a city in India will absorb the opinions and evaluative fads of cultural celebrities in New York. The danger is that everyone everywhere will come to think the same things and hold the same values, often in ways which don't even make sense given their particular context—what the New Yorker might care about need not always be what the Austrian or Indian should focus their attention on. Moreover, because of this homogenization, it might become more and more difficult for people who think differently to find suitable environments to escape the world-culture.

Now there is a sense in which the internet and social media actually foster the development of a myriad of subcultures. For example, there are a plethora of communities of enthusiasts of various kinds, each with its own influencers. You can find groups devoted to indie music, particular exercise regimens, fish-keeping, knitting, and much else. However, this is a superficial form of diversity that might obscure deeper patterns of conformity and homogeneity. Most of us participate in social media that isn't simply limited to such subcultures, and society-wide influencers (famous authors, intellectuals, celebrities, CEOs) increasingly frame and opine on the issues of the day in predictable and concordant ways. Because of these features of the online landscape, the dangers for homogeneity in terms of fundamental empirical and evaluative assumptions about society are all the more pressing.

Mill worried about increasing homogeneity in his own time in the mid-to-late 19th century. People were being brought under one common influence through the rapid development of trade. Newspapers played an important role in the homogenization of opinion, as did formal education. "Formerly, different ranks, different neighborhoods, different trades and professions, lived in what might be called different worlds . . . they now read the same things, listen to the same things, see the same things," wrote Mill. In order to combat this homogenization, he thought, people must consciously come to embrace social norms that prize diversity of thought and expression. Otherwise, "if resistance waits till life is reduced nearly to one uniform type, all deviations from that type will come to be considered impious, immoral, even monstrous."[49]

Now, in democratic countries, cultural homogenization is not *directed*. At many points in recent history, it was. People living under the regimes of Stalin or Hitler were all supposed to think the same things and want the same things. And this was enforced top-down by these regimes through harsh sanctions for deviation. Furthermore, the regimes consciously decided what propaganda to disseminate to the masses. But just because there is little by way of such top-down, consciously engineered, cultural homogenization within modern democracies, we shouldn't conclude that it isn't taking place or that it isn't detrimental. The homogenization can be a *spontaneous* order, so that each individual responding to the incentives they have can act in a way so as to move the culture towards a particular equilibrium.[50]

Independent thought is hard to cultivate in this equilibrium because there is nowhere to flee. And though historical thinkers and writers can often be a rich treasure trove for exploring ways of thinking differently, the equilibrium culture will consider them as problematic or crazy insofar as they disagree with modern values and assumptions. Thus, even if a wealth of wisdom exists in this way, it will be *untouchable*. As Nietzsche puts it though Zarathustra:

> "No shepherd and one herd! Everybody wants the same, everybody is the same: whoever feels different goes voluntarily into a madhouse.
>
> "'Formerly, all the world was mad,' say the most refined, and they blink.[51]

One can't help but notice these patterns (perhaps on steroids, so to speak) in our own culture today: the ceaseless homogenization of thought, though undirected by any "shepherd," and the disavowal of great past thinkers whose values and perspectives the most educated and sophisticated people find quaint or worse.

> It is good, from time to time, to view the present as already past, and to examine what elements it contains that will add to the world's store of permanent possessions, that will live and give life when we and all our generation have perished. In the light of this contemplation, all human experience is transformed, and whatever is sordid or personal is purged away.
>
> —Bertrand Russell, *On History*

Philosopher Samuel Scheffler asks us to consider the following thought experiment. Suppose you learn that 30 days after your death, humanity will be wiped out by a giant asteroid. How would this change your attitudes towards your own life? How would it change what you find valuable and meaningful to do? Would it alter what you find pleasant or fulfilling? Scheffler thinks that the thought experiment reveals a great deal about our values and what sustains them.[1]

Notice a crucial feature of the case: your life is not to be shortened in any way. We can imagine that an evil demon has programmed things so that whenever you die, say at time t, the asteroid will hit at t+30 days. Hence, whatever dread or despair you feel cannot be about *your* death.

But even if your life has not been shortened, presumably much of what you find meaningful now would lose its value. Would you still gain as much satisfaction from your job? Would you still want to create new things—write a novel, build a beautiful house, design a new product people might use? It would seem natural to wonder "What's the point of it all?"

Now, the very goals of some of our projects depend on humanity's future. And so, of course, we won't see the point in pursuing them if we learn about the asteroid. For example, imagine you are a cancer researcher and the idea you're working on will likely take decades to be brought to fruition. If you expect that the cure will only come after your death, then naturally there is no point in pursuing the research, since the asteroid is going to kill everyone soon after your death anyway. Similarly, you might not choose to have any (or any more) children if you know they're going to die via asteroid.

But Scheffler thinks the despair goes deeper than that. Even with respect to projects that do not depend on the future of humanity after our deaths for their successful culmination, we will likely find that they have lost value. For example, it would seem relatively pointless to develop a new skill or explore a new literature, even though one's ability to do these things does not depend on what happens after one dies. Likewise, it would seem pointless for many to work on writing a new software program or building a bridge. It would seem pointless to compete in a marathon. And much else. Perhaps the only things we'd still find worthwhile are the basic pleasures of life: tasty food, sex, video entertainment, etc. Though maybe even these things will lose some of their luster. Many might choose to live the rest of their lives in a drug-fueled stupor.

If all this is right, then it seems that the future of humanity (what Scheffler calls the "afterlife") is an essential condition for things mattering to us. Many of our practices of valuing presuppose that humanity has a future, and that there is something to pass on even as we pass away. On the other hand, the prospect of our own death doesn't have this effect on us. We all know that we're going to die at some point. We might well fear death, but it doesn't induce the same kind of nihilism in us that the doomsday scenario would.

In fact, Scheffler argues, although we fear death, death is in a way a background condition for things to matter to us as they do. Many of the evaluative attitudes we have towards life presuppose *stages* of life and hence presuppose death. For example, we might value doing well in school, but that assumes being in a stage of life when one is in school. Likewise, the way we look at professional success, relationships, and so much more is indexed to the stage of life we're at. If we think through what it would mean to be immortal on this earth, we might find that it would be a life of intolerable alienation and boredom. So, paradoxically, both our deaths and the future continuance of humanity (the afterlife) are conditions for things mattering to us as they do.

Now, it might be tempting to think that the only reason we feel nihilism and despair about the t+30d asteroid is that it will kill many of our friends and loved ones. But it is easy to alter the case so that it abstracts away from these considerations. Thus, Scheffler asks us to imagine an infertility scenario, where everyone suddenly becomes infertile. Hence, suppose that from now on, there will be no more human babies born. But this means that the people we care about won't die prematurely like in the asteroid case. All our friends and loved ones will be able to live out the course of their natural lives. Nonetheless, the nihilism remains. Does the infertility scenario cure the feelings of nihilism that the asteroid case induced in you (if it did)?[2]

What this suggests is that the meaning of our lives is *essentially dependent* on the continuing existence of future human beings, whom we do not and cannot know.[3] In this way, the meaning of a life depends on its context within the history of humanity as a whole—just as the purpose of a brushstroke or word or note is only to be understood within the context of a painting or book or symphony. A stray, isolated brushstroke, word, or note is meaningless. The great symphony of human existence must continue. It is often emphasized that future generations are dependent on us in important ways—on whether we leave them with enough savings, a habitable climate, and so on. But what's not emphasized is that *we* are also dependent on *them* for the very meaning of our lives.

SIMPLE CONTINUATION VS FLOURISHING

Though Scheffler doesn't emphasize this, I believe it's not only the mere continuation of humanity but also its future flourishing that we care about. We want there to be prosperous individuals and cultures in the future. We want there to exist human virtue, innovation, great art and literature, and thriving communities.

To see this, let's modify Scheffler's thought experiment a bit. Take whatever you think constitutes the lack of human flourishing. I suspect people will differ as to what they think of as flourishing individuals and cultures. But imagine now that instead of a post-mortem asteroid, there's a post-mortem cessation of human flourishing. So, substitute for 'human flourishing' whatever that term means for you, and imagine that after your death, though the human species will continue on, it will be utterly devoid of human flourishing, forever.

Here we can use our imaginations and employ whatever dystopian scenarios we can think of. Maybe humanity returns to a dark age under strict dictatorial control—an Orwellian 1984 scenario, say, but everywhere and forever. Or imagine that a mind virus destroys human creativity and intelligence, making people turn into quasi-zombies. Or imagine a scenario where an evil scientist genetically modifies all humans to maximize their violence and cruelty and to possess little by way of the noble human traits and dispositions. Or imagine the dystopia painted in Kurt Vonnegut's short story, "Harrison Bergeron."

I suspect the only reason we may not immediately become as nihilistic when faced with such imagined futures, as compared to the post-mortem asteroid, is that we hold out some form of hope. Maybe eventually humanity will recover in some way. Or, while most of the world becomes a dystopia, a small country or community or rebel stronghold somewhere carries on the torch of human flourishing—as often happens in dystopian fiction. But if we stipulate that the future is a forever-dark age, then it seems to me that our nihilism will come back. What's the point of it all? Hence, the meaningfulness of our lives, here and now, depends on whether humanity will exist and flourish in the future. This has tremendous implications for how we should think of speaking our minds, which I will turn to presently.

TAKING STOCK

In this book, I have argued that social pressures can create dangerous blind spots. In order to combat these blind spots, courageous individuals must share their evidence and offer different perspectives, precisely in those contexts where the social pressure exists. Individuals must do their part in maintaining the "epistemic commons" in this way, even in the presence of social costs. Indeed, morality often demands us to sacrifice, to some extent, our narrow self-interest for the common good.

In the past two chapters, I have claimed that what might look like costs to self-interest may not actually be costs when we take a broader perspective on what makes human life worth living. What makes human life fundamentally worth living is not pleasure or social status. This is not to say that we should *avoid* pleasure or social status. In general, it is good for us to have these things, insofar as they contribute to whatever it is that makes life worthwhile. But if seeking these things in a particular context comes at a cost to whatever it is that makes life worthwhile, then seeking pleasure or status in such a context is counterproductive even for our own sakes.

What is it that makes life worth living? One answer, which the ancient Greek philosophers emphasized in particular, was explored in Chapter 4. A good life, on this view, consists in the development and excellent exercise of our distinctively human capacities—namely, our rational faculties. But in order to do so, we must speak our minds. For reasoning is an *essentially social* activity; we simply cannot do it well alone, no matter how smart we are.

Another perspective, which we get from John Stuart Mill and Friedrich Nietzsche (among others), is that a good (or great) life must exhibit independence. Not just superficial independence—of taste in food, clothing, music—but *evaluative* independence. Great human beings, according to these philosophers, don't just go with the crowd when it comes to the fundamental assumptions of society. They don't pick their views on justice, say, according to the fashion of their milieu. Rather, they are able to think for themselves, maybe not on every single issue (who has the time?), but at least on the important things. Yet, to cultivate this independence and let it thrive, I said, we must speak our minds. Again, sacrificing independence for pleasure and social status is perverse on this view.

Perhaps these ideas are quaint. Maybe you don't agree. Perhaps rationality is not what makes humans special. Maybe it is love or friendship. And it could be that independence is overrated. A life of athletic achievement, say, along with robust family and community relationships could be a well-lived life even if it contains little by way of independent thought. Nietzsche and Mill were somewhat quirky fellows, and so of course they'd think "independence" is what it's all about! Ultimately, these worries may have something to them, and I don't want to pretend to settle the matter here.

However, you might have found plausible the idea that social pressure creates blind spots. It is also hard to deny that each culture and age has had its follies—just open a history book! It is exceedingly implausible that *we*, here and now, are not missing the big picture on *something*—that our culture doesn't have blind spots it's not even aware of. The crusaders, the witch burners, the 17th century Catholic Church—all failed to appreciate their huge blind spots. And we are humans just like them.

When reflecting on what future generations will judge us badly for, it is tempting to grasp at things already alive in the zeitgeist. If you talk to people about this, many will likely mention the fact that we allowed climate change to happen so drastically. Or, some will think of our large factory farms. Yet these things, terrible as they are, are not *blind spots* of our culture. Thousands and thousands of articles, books, and think-pieces are written on them constantly. These issues are very much alive in the zeitgeist. The blind spots, on the other hand, are what the dominant cultural forces cannot or will not allow themselves to even think of.

Here's an example. Imagine time traveling to Salem, Massachusetts, circa 1692 and asking a local magistrate whether he might have a blind spot and whether the future will judge him harshly. He would likely respond, "Yes, it is possible. We might be hanging the wrong person. Perhaps this other woman is the *real* witch." He won't even be able or willing to think (out loud, anyway) "Maybe there are no witches." This, of course, is definitely not to suggest that climate change and factory farming are not moral problems. But there might be equally big or even bigger issues that we can't even think about. That's why they're blind spots. To look for blind spots, we must look at where the social pressure is. In Salem, if you didn't believe in witches you might be accused of being a heretic or perhaps a witch yourself. So, there would have been enormous pressure not to deny the existence of witches.

But blind spots threaten the future of humanity—both in terms of its existence and its flourishing. Moreover, there are advantages that peoples throughout history have had, which we increasingly do not. For one, many of their errors only affected their circumscribed contexts. The crusaders had no effect on people living in China. And while women in China suffered from foot binding for centuries, the practice had no effect on women in India. There was a great variety of cultures so that even if one turned repressive, people could still flourish elsewhere. During the European dark ages, for instance, science and philosophy still flourished elsewhere in the world— particularly, the Middle East and Asia. The more our global culture homogenizes, however, the less scope there is for this kind of thing to happen. All our eggs are increasingly in one cultural basket.

Second, the pace of technological and social change has quickened drastically. Life in the 6th century was different, but not that different, from life in the 5th for the average person. The difference between life for the average person in 12,100 BC and 12,000 BC is even smaller. But the difference between now and one hundred years ago is *huge*—just read an early Hemingway or Fitzgerald novel (and those don't even capture the representative person, who at the time, was a subsistence farmer or shepherd without electricity somewhere). In more or less any domain, the rate of change humanity has seen has been exponential, not linear. And so, given the dramatic rate of change we see now, we can mess things up pretty badly if we're not careful.

SPEAK (YOUR MIND) NOW, OR FOREVER HOLD YOUR PEACE

If all this is right, then there are two chief upshots. First, there is a good reason to resist the homogenization of culture. And one way we can do this as individuals is to speak our minds and to create: new ideas, new perspectives, new institutions. We can refuse to go along with the cultural herd. This is but one moment in the history of humanity, and the ideals of today do not have some special authority simply by virtue of being *today's* ideals. By speaking, writing, giving our own perspectives, we may well contribute something of lasting value, something that future cultures can draw upon—*even* if we are ignored (or worse) today.

The second implication is that we should do what we can to avoid mass blind spots, because these can threaten the future existence and flourishing of humanity. We should do what we can to avoid a global Chernobyl, so to speak. But that means sharing evidence even when there is social pressure not to do so—individuals not sharing their evidence is *precisely* what leads to Chernobyl-type scenarios. It also means doing what we can to make it less costly for dissenters to put their evidence on the table, even if we don't have special information of our own to share in a particular context.

Of course, because we live here and now, the costs to our social status loom large. But if the earlier arguments are on the right track, then the meaning of one's life is only to be understood by looking at the full tapestry of human existence. If we reflect on this, trying to imagine the tapestry as a whole, then the utter insignificance of a little social approval and disapproval here or there becomes apparent. What do *not* become insignificant are the lasting contributions we made while we were here, and the ways in which we shaped the future of humanity.

Indeed, when we look at the past, the costs we stand to face look trivial. Think of teenage boys sent to fight in the gruesome, disease-filled trenches of World War I, often to be mowed down by machine guns. What is the difference between 94 "likes" as opposed to 11, when compared to what they sacrificed? Or think of the fact that for most of human history people lived in conditions where they never got to read, could expect to die before the age of 30 from simple bacterial infections, and lost half their children before the age of five. Without these past people we wouldn't be here and we wouldn't have the relatively extraordinary comforts of modern life. We sit lazily on their shoulders. But if we reflect on history, we can appreciate that whatever we stand to lose by going against the crowd is miniscule. Being born now, as opposed to a century or millennium earlier, is an enormous privilege—one we should be grateful for and make the best use of.

Moreover, if we reflect carefully on our values, we can see that most things matter to us only on the condition that humanity flourishes in the future. This need not be *all* of humanity—it is inevitable that many future people will lead bad lives. But we need *some* glimmers of light *somewhere* in the future-tapestry of humanity for life and all its striving to be worth it. To preserve these glimmers, we need to be constantly vigilant against cultural blind spots, an all-too-common occurrence throughout history, made vastly more potent now because of the pace of change and the homogenization of culture. And the only way we as individuals can do this is to speak our minds, and dare to think differently.

So, it's OK to think differently. It's OK to speak your mind. In fact, you should. Far too much hangs in the balance.

Notes

PROLOGUE

1. Mill, *On Liberty and Other Essays*, 37.
2. Russell, "Free Thought and Official Propaganda," 13.

THE EPISTEMIC COMMONS

1. Smith, *An Inquiry into the Nature and Causes of the Wealth of Nations.*
2. Sloman and Fernbach, *The Knowledge Illusion*, 121.
3. Rozenblit and Keil, "The Misunderstood Limits of Folk Science: An Illusion of Explanatory Depth"; Lawson, "The Science of Cycology: Failures to Understand How Everyday Objects Work."
4. Clifford, "The Ethics of Belief," 292.
5. This idea was first introduced in Hardin, "The Tragedy of the Commons."
6. Anderson, Hildreth, and Howland, "Is the Desire for Status a Fundamental Human Motive? A Review of the Empirical Literature."
7. Empirical work suggests that in general, when deliberating, groups tend to focus on commonly known information as opposed to information possessed only by some individuals within the group. This can cause the group to make poor decisions. See: Stasser and Titus, "Pooling of Unshared Information in Group Decision Making: Biased Information Sampling During Discussion"; Hightower and Sayeed, "The Impact of Computer-Mediated Communication Systems on Biased Group Discussion"; Stasser, Abele, and Parsons, "Information Flow and Influence in Collective Choice"; Sunstein and Hastie, *Wiser: Getting Beyond Groupthink to Make Groups Smarter*. Part of the explanation here is that sharing unique information tends to carry social costs; see: Stasser and Titus, "Hidden Profiles: A Brief History." The problem becomes worse as the group size increases.
8. Parts of the presentation are fictionalized for dramatic purposes, but the core features of the events are preserved.
9. For more on this, see: Sunstein, *Conformity*.

10. Gulick, *Administrative Reflections from World War II*, 125.

11. For further analysis of the fiasco, see: Janis, *Groupthink*; Sunstein and Hastie, *Wiser: Getting Beyond Groupthink to Make Groups Smarter*.

12. Bicchieri, *Norms in the Wild*, 19.

13. For more on why such strategies of vindicating the partisan face significant challenges, see: Joshi, "What Are the Chances You're Right about Everything? An Epistemic Challenge for Modern Partisanship."

14. The worry is not merely theoretical. For instance, a recent poll shows that 62% of Americans say they have political opinions they are afraid to share, and 32% worry about potential lost job opportunities if their political views become known; see: Jenkins, "Poll: 62% of Americans Say They Have Political Views They're Afraid to Share." Another study shows that the proportion of Americans who do not feel that they can speak their minds has *tripled* from the height of McCarthyism and the Red Scare of the 1950s: Gibson and Sutherland, "Keeping Your Mouth Shut: Spiraling Self-Censorship in the United States." The study further finds that the tendency to self-censor increases with level of education.

15. Noelle-Neumann, "The Spiral of Silence: A Theory of Public Opinion."

16. For a thorough recent treatment of how individuals should regulate their epistemic lives in the potential presence of epistemic defeaters, see: Ballantyne, *Knowing Our Limits*.

17. Sunstein, *Conformity*, 7.

18. Bowles and Gintis, *A Cooperative Species*.

19. Sunstein, *Conformity*, 7.

20. For an exploration of "Galilean personalities" in the context of modern science, see: Dreger, *Galileo's Middle Finger: Heretics, Activists, and One Scholar's Search for Justice*.

21. Straightforwardly so at least on one interpretation of quantum mechanics. The other interpretations, however, are even more counterintuitive. For more on the interpretive issues, see: Maudlin, *Philosophy of Physics: Quantum Theory*.

22. See: Maudlin, *Philosophy of Physics: Space and Time*. One notorious persisting problem here is that quantum mechanics and general relativity do not cohere. So, the search for a unified theory continues.

23. Sloman and Fernbach, *The Knowledge Illusion*, 224.

24. Mill, *On Liberty and Other Essays*, 26.

25. Longino, *Science as Social Knowledge*, 74.

26. For a short but comprehensive overview of the field, see: Finlay, "Four Faces of Moral Realism."

27. For example, the late Derek Parfit, a non-naturalist, was a renowned professor at All Souls College, Oxford. But Peter Railton and Michael Smith, both metaethical naturalists, hold professorships at the University of Michigan and Princeton University respectively, and are similarly well-regarded in the profession. Other prominent metaethicists

include Sharon Street at NYU and Christine Korsgaard at Harvard who defend constructivism, Mark Schroeder at USC who defends Humeanism, and Allan Gibbard (emeritus) at Michigan who has defended expressivism. Though, my colleague Kevin Vallier thinks that divine command theory often gets short shrift in the teaching and research practices of the field.

28. Loury, "Self-Censorship in Public Discourse," 452.

29. Loury, 453.

A DUTY TO SPEAK YOUR MIND

1. Kahan et al., "Motivated Numeracy and Enlightened Self-Government," 77. See also: Kahan, "Why We Are Poles Apart on Climate Change."

2. See for example: Downs, "An Economic Theory of Political Action in a Democracy"; Caplan, *The Myth of the Rational Voter*; Brennan, *Against Democracy*.

3. This notion of *prima facie* duty is introduced in Ross, *The Right and the Good*.

4. Pipes, *Communism: A History*.

5. Kant, "Groundwork of The Metaphysics of Morals."

6. Lackey, "The Duty to Object," 15.

7. Sunstein, *Conformity*, 11. Sunstein here cites Sunstein, Hastie, and Schkade, "What Happened on Deliberation Day?"

8. Kelly, "Evidence: Fundamental Concepts and the Phenomenal Conception," 942.

9. One issue here is that sometimes we may share evidence for a claim in good faith, but nonetheless be mistaken about whether what we are sharing is in fact evidence for the claim in question. Honest conspiracy theorists of certain stripes will presumably fit this bill. The worry about the duty presented here is that the more we include a "factive" element—namely a requirement that the evidence E shared in support of some proposition P *actually be* evidence for P—the less the duty becomes action-guiding. This is because we can be mistaken about what counts as evidence for what. On the other hand, unless we include some kind of reasonableness constraint on what is given as evidence for what, the duty asks honest conspiracy theorists to share their views. This is a dilemma, and I am inclined to bite the latter bullet so as not to impose an objective reasonableness constraint. But it's a dilemma for any view within regulative epistemology or the ethics of expression. For instance it will be an issue for the account defended in Lackey, "The Duty to Object." Should we object only when we know or justifiably believe, as opposed to simply believe? How can we tell? In other ways it's a problem for the view in Fantl, *The Limitations of the Open Mind*. The idea there is that we shouldn't engage open-mindedly with an argument which

we know yields a false conclusion. But it's not easy to tell the difference between what we know and what we merely believe.

10. Shi et al., "The Wisdom of Polarized Crowds"; Hong and Page, "Groups of Diverse Problem Solvers Can Outperform Groups of High-Ability Problem Solvers."

11. Mill, *On Liberty and Other Essays*, 60–61.

12. Tappin and McKay, "The Illusion of Moral Superiority"; Dunning, "False Moral Superiority"; Dunning and Epley, "Feeling 'Holier than Thou': Are Self-Serving Assessments Produced by Errors in Self- or Social Prediction?"

13. Aristotle, *Nicomachean Ethics*, III.7, 1115b. (Following standard practice, all references to Aristotle are based on Bekker numbers, rather than page numbers.)

14. Aristotle seems to suggest that courage is only manifested in cases where there is a danger of death; see: Aristotle, III.6, 1115a10-30. Though, we presumably need not follow him that far.

15. Aristotle, III.9, 1117a.

16. See: Mankiw, *Principles of Economics*; Krugman and Wells, *Microeconomics*.

17. For more on public goods and associated problems, see: Anomaly, "Public Goods and Government Action."

18. Smith, *An Inquiry into the Nature and Causes of the Wealth of Nations*, 570–71.

19. Cf. Mueller, *Public Choice III*.

20. A Nash equilibrium is a situation where no individual has an incentive to change their strategy. Rational individuals (on the decision-theoretic conception of 'rational') will choose their strategies so that the resulting situation is a Nash equilibrium. See, e.g.: Binmore, *Game Theory: A Very Short Introduction*.

21. The historical context and the interaction between Galileo and the Catholic Church are more complex than I can do justice to here. For a detailed recent biography, see: Wootton, *Galileo: Watcher of the Skies*.

22. For some examples of putative cases of such dynamics within modern social science, see: Pinker, *The Blank Slate*; Jussim, *Social Perception and Social Reality: Why Accuracy Dominates Bias and Self-Fulfilling Prophecy*; Duarte et al., "Political Diversity Will Improve Social Psychological Science"; Dreger, *Galileo's Middle Finger: Heretics, Activists, and One Scholar's Search for Justice*.

CHALLENGES AND TEMPTATIONS

1. See, for example: Kagan, "Do I Make a Difference?"; Nefsky, "How You Can Help, without Making a Difference."

2. Asch, "Opinions and Social Pressure."

3. Asch, 32.

4. Cross and Tiller, "Judicial Partisanship and Obedience to Legal Doctrine"; Sunstein, *Conformity*.

5. Andersen, "The Emperor's New Clothes," 57.
6. Kuran, *Private Truths, Public Lies*; Bicchieri, *Norms in the Wild*.
7. Bicchieri, *Norms in the Wild*; Bicchieri, *The Grammar of Society*.
8. Kuran, *Private Truths, Public Lies*; Willer, Kuwabara, and Macy, "The False Enforcement of Unpopular Norms."
9. Noelle-Neumann, "The Spiral of Silence: A Theory of Public Opinion"; Noelle-Neumann, *The Spiral of Silence*.
10. Bicchieri, *The Grammar of Society*, 205.
11. For a model of how this might occur, see: Kuran, *Private Truths, Public Lies*, 56–57.
12. Mill, *On Liberty and Other Essays*, 58.
13. For further discussion, see: Dreger, *Galileo's Middle Finger: Heretics, Activists, and One Scholar's Search for Justice*.
14. For a discussion on the role of sacred objects in a range of cultures, see: Haidt, *The Righteous Mind*.
15. Mill, *On Liberty and Other Essays*, 27.
16. Mill, 23.
17. Mill, 33.
18. I owe this term to Daniel Wolt.
19. Tosi and Warmke, *Grandstanding: The Use and Abuse of Moral Talk*, 51–52.
20. One reason for this dynamic is the "black sheep" effect—people are more hostile towards deviant members of the in-group as opposed to members of the outgroup. Thus, there is a need to demonstrate loyalty to the group's values by ratcheting up in this way. See: Marques, Yzerbyt, and Leyens, "The 'Black Sheep Effect': Extremity of Judgments towards Ingroup Members as a Function of Group Identification."
21. For great overviews of the literature see: Simler and Hanson, *The Elephant in the Brain*; Trivers, *The Folly of Fools: The Logic of Deceit and Self-Deception in Human Life*.
22. For more on this phenomenon, see: Festinger, "Cognitive Dissonance." See also: Kuran, *Private Truths, Public Lies*.
23. Orwell, *1984*, 281.
24. Ostrom, "Collective Action and the Evolution of Social Norms."

DEVELOPING AS A THINKER

1. Kuran, *Private Truths, Public Lies*.
2. Nietzsche, "Twilight of the Idols," Maxims and Arrows, 12. (Following standard practice, all references to Nietzsche's corpus are based on section number, rather than page number.)
3. Aristotle, *Nicomachean Ethics*, I.5, 1095b.
4. For a modern defense of this kind of view of ethics, see: Thomson, *Normativity*.
5. For more on this, see: Kraut, *Aristotle on the Human Good*.

6. Aristotle, *Nicomachean Ethics*, I.5, 1095b.

7. The ancient Greek philosophers often defend a subtler view: human excellence, whatever it may be, *makes* pleasure and social status good for us.

8. Silver et al., "Mastering the Game of Go without Human Knowledge."

9. Shiffrin, *Speech Matters: On Lying, Morality, and the Law*, 87–88.

10. Shiffrin, 89–90.

11. See for example: Heron, "The Pathology of Boredom"; Arrigo and Bullock, "The Psychological Effects of Solitary Confinement on Prisoners in Supermax Units: Reviewing What We Know and Recommending What Should Change."; Gawande, "Hellhole."

12. Plato, "Apology," 29 d-e. (Following standard practice, all references to Plato are based on Stephanus numbers, rather than page numbers.)

13. Plato, 30b.

14. Plato, 36b.

15. Plato, 38a.

16. Latane and Rodin, "A Lady in Distress: Inhibiting Effects of Friends and Strangers on Bystander Intervention."

17. Hall, Johansson, and Strandberg, "Lifting the Veil of Morality: Choice Blindness and Attitude Reversals on a Self-Transforming Survey."

18. Mercier and Sperber, *The Enigma of Reason*, 253.

19. See: Mynatt, Doherty, and Tweney, "Confirmation Bias in a Simulated Research Environment: An Experimental Study of Scientific Inference"; Wason, "Reasoning about a Rule."

20. Taber and Lodge, "Motivated Skepticism in the Evaluation of Political Beliefs."

21. West, Meserve, and Stanovich, "Cognitive Sophistication Does Not Attenuate the Bias Blind Spot."

22. Trouche et al., "The Selective Laziness of Reasoning."

23. Mercier and Sperber, *The Enigma of Reason*, 236.

24. Hastie, Penrod, and Pennington, *Inside the Jury*.

25. See: Janis, *Groupthink*; Sunstein, *Conformity*.

26. Russell, "The Best Answer to Fanaticism—Liberalism."

INDEPENDENCE AND THE GOOD LIFE

1. Kant, "An Answer to the Question: What Is Enlightenment?," 17. The comparison to one of Nietzsche's early essays is striking:

> But what is it that constrains the individual to fear his neighbour, to think and act like a member of a herd, and to have no joy in himself? Modesty, perhaps, in a few rare cases. With the great majority it is indolence, inertia, in short that tendency to laziness of which the traveller spoke. He is right: men are even lazier than they are timid, and fear most of all the inconveniences with which unconditional honesty and nakedness would burden them . . . When the great thinker

despises mankind, he despises its laziness: for it is on account of their laziness that men seem like factory products, things of no consequence and unworthy to be associated with or instructed.

(Nietzsche, "Schopenhauer as Educator," 1.)

For more on the similarities and differences between the philosophical projects of Kant and Nietzsche, see: Ridley, *Nietzsche's Conscience*.

2. Mill, *On Liberty and Other Essays*, 71.
3. Part of the challenge here is to make sense of how independence could be good in itself for Mill, given his defense of utilitarianism. This raises subtle issues, but nonetheless, his defense of individuality as good in itself is quite clear in *On Liberty*, Chapter 3. For more discussion on this, see: Donner, "Mill on Individuality."
4. Mill, *On Liberty and Other Essays*, 63.
5. Mill, 73.
6. Mill, 66–67.
7. Mill, 70.
8. See, for example: Nietzsche, *Beyond Good and Evil*, 260, 261; Nietzsche, "Thus Spoke Zarathustra," Part I, On the Tree on the Mountainside.
9. Cf. Nehamas, *Nietzsche: Life as Literature*.
10. Nietzsche, *Beyond Good and Evil*, 212.
11. One value that Nietzsche often challenged is equality. For a small sampling, see: Nietzsche, "Thus Spoke Zarathustra," Part II, 7, 16; Nietzsche, *Beyond Good and Evil*, 62; Nietzsche, *The Gay Science*, 18, 377; Nietzsche, "The Antichrist," 57.
12. Nietzsche, "The Antichrist," Preface.
13. Nietzsche, *The Gay Science*, 283.
14. Cf. Huddleston, *Nietzsche on the Decadence and Flourishing of Culture*.
15. Nietzsche describes these dangers poignantly in one of his early essays, on Schopenhauer. He writes:

These people who have fled inward for their freedom also have to live outwardly, become visible, let themselves be seen; they are united with mankind through countless ties of blood, residence, education, fatherland, chance, the importunity of others; they are likewise supposed to harbor countless opinions simply because they are the ruling opinions of the time; every gesture which is not clearly a denial counts as agreement; every motion of the hand that does not destroy is interpreted as approval. They know, these solitaries, free in spirit, that they continually seem other than what they think: while they desire nothing but truth and honesty, they are encompassed by a net of misunderstandings.

(Nietzsche, "Schopenhauer as Educator," 3.)

See also Nietzsche, "Twilight of the Idols," Skirmishes, 17.
16. Cf. Reginster, *The Affirmation of Life*.
17. Nietzsche, *The Gay Science*, 3.

18. Nietzsche, 3.
19. Nietzsche, *Beyond Good and Evil*, 43. See also: Nietzsche, *The Gay Science*, 308.
20. Nietzsche, "Thus Spoke Zarathustra," Part I, 1.
21. Nietzsche, Part I, 9.
22. Nietzsche, Part III, 26.
23. Nietzsche, *Beyond Good and Evil*, 29.
24. Nietzsche, *The Gay Science*, 2. See also: Nietzsche, "Twilight of the Idols," Skirmishes, 18.
25. Mill, *On Liberty and Other Essays*, 68.
26. In fact, for Nietzsche, it is impossible that every person can be great within a society; greatness is possible only for a few, in part because greatness is essentially contrastive. He talks for example about high culture being a "pyramid" which rests on a base of mediocrity; see: Nietzsche, "The Antichrist," 57. For thorough discussion on this issue, see: Huddleston, *Nietzsche on the Decadence and Flourishing of Culture*.
27. Mill, *On Liberty and Other Essays*, 72.
28. Mill, 42–43.
29. Nietzsche, "The Dawn," 297.
30. Nietzsche, "Schopenhauer as Educator," 3.
31. Nietzsche, "Thus Spoke Zarathustra," Part II, 16. See also: Nietzsche, *The Gay Science*, 366.
32. For an explication of the distinction as he conceives it, see: Nietzsche, *Beyond Good and Evil*, 211.
33. Nietzsche, "Human, All-Too-Human," 579.
34. For a recent defense of ignoring politics, see: Freiman, *Why It's OK to Ignore Politics*.
35. Nietzsche, "The Antichrist," Preface.
36. Nietzsche, *The Gay Science*, 174.
37. Huddleston, *Nietzsche on the Decadence and Flourishing of Culture*.
38. Mill, *On Liberty and Other Essays*, 56.
39. Cf. Huddleston, *Nietzsche on the Decadence and Flourishing of Culture*.
40. For a helpful and detailed discussion on the scope of his critique, see: Leiter, *Nietzsche on Morality*.
41. Nietzsche, *Beyond Good and Evil*, 227.
42. Nietzsche, 30.
43. He says in his autobiography of sorts, "How much truth can a spirit *endure*, how much truth does it *dare*? More and more that became for me the real measure of value." (Nietzsche, "Ecce Homo," Preface, 3.) Though, Nietzsche has complex views about the "will to truth" in general. See, for example: Gemes, "Nietzsche's Critique of Truth."
44. Nietzsche, "On the Genealogy of Morals," Essay III, 19. He says there:

    Our educated people of today, our "good people," do not tell lies—that is true; but that is *not* to their credit! A real lie, a genuine, resolute, "honest" lie (on whose value one should consult Plato) would be something far too severe and potent for them: it would demand of them what one *may* not demand of them, that they should open their eyes to themselves, that they should know how to distinguish "true" and "false" in themselves. All they are capable of is a *dishonest* lie; whoever today accounts himself a "good man" is utterly incapable of confronting any matter except with *dishonest mendaciousness*—a mendaciousness that is abysmal but innocent, truehearted, blue-eyed, and virtuous.

45. Nietzsche, "Human, All-Too-Human," 483.
46. Nietzsche, "The Antichrist," 54.
47. Nietzsche, "Twilight of the Idols," Skirmishes, 18.
48. Mill, *On Liberty and Other Essays*, 39.
49. Mill, 82.
50. For more on social norms and spontaneous order, see: Anomaly and Brennan, "Social Norms, the Invisible Hand, and the Law."
51. Nietzsche, "Thus Spoke Zarathustra," Part I, 5.

EPILOGUE

1. Scheffler, *Death and the Afterlife*.
2. This scenario is the subject of *The Children of Men*, a 1992 novel by P.D. James, later adapted into a movie.
3. Or at least, future sentient creatures with goals and desires like ours.

References

Andersen, Hans Christian. "The Emperor's New Clothes." In *Hans Christian Andersen's Complete Fairy Tales*, translated by Jean Pierre Hersholt. San Diego, CA: Canterbury Classics, 2014.

Anderson, Cameron, John Angus Hildreth, and Laura Howland. "Is the Desire for Status a Fundamental Human Motive? A Review of the Empirical Literature." *Psychological Bulletin* 141, no. 3 (2015): 574–601.

Anomaly, Jonathan. "Public Goods and Government Action." *Politics, Philosophy & Economics* 14, no. 2 (2015): 109–28.

Anomaly, Jonathan, and Geoffrey Brennan. "Social Norms, the Invisible Hand, and the Law." *The University of Queensland Law Journal* 33, no. 2 (2014): 263–83.

Aristotle. *Nicomachean Ethics*. Translated by Terence Irwin. 2nd ed. Indianapolis, IN: Hackett Publishing, 1999.

Arrigo, Bruce A., and Jennifer Leslie Bullock. "The Psychological Effects of Solitary Confinement on Prisoners in Supermax Units: Reviewing What We Know and Recommending What Should Change." *International Journal of Offender Therapy and Comparative Criminology* 52, no. 6 (2008): 622–40.

Asch, Solomon E. "Opinions and Social Pressure." *Scientific American* 193, no. 5 (November 1, 1955): 31–35. https://doi.org/10.1038/scientificamerican1155-31.

Ballantyne, Nathan. *Knowing Our Limits*. New York: Oxford University Press, 2019.

Bicchieri, Cristina. *The Grammar of Society*. New York: Cambridge University Press, 2006.

———. *Norms in the Wild*. New York: Oxford University Press, 2017.

Binmore, Ken. *Game Theory: A Very Short Introduction*. Oxford: Oxford University Press, 2007.

Bowles, Samuel, and Herbert Gintis. *A Cooperative Species: Human Reciprocity and Its Evolution*. Princeton University Press, 2011.

Brennan, Jason. *Against Democracy*. Princeton, NJ: Princeton University Press, 2016.

Caplan, Bryan. *The Myth of the Rational Voter*. Princeton, NJ: Princeton University Press, 2008.

Clifford, W.K. "The Ethics of Belief." *Contemporary Review* 29 (1877): 289–309.

Cross, Frank, and Emerson Tiller. "Judicial Partisanship and Obedience to Legal Doctrine." *The Yale Law Journal* 107, no. 7 (1998): 2155–76.

Donner, Wendy. "Mill on Individuality." In *A Companion to Mill*, edited by Christopher Macleod and Dale E. Miller. Malden, MA: Wiley-Blackwell, 2017.

Downs, Anthony. "An Economic Theory of Political Action in a Democracy." *Journal of Political Economy* 65, no. 2 (1957): 135–50.

Dreger, Alice. *Galileo's Middle Finger: Heretics, Activists, and One Scholar's Search for Justice*. New York: Penguin Books, 2015.

Duarte, José, Jarret Crawford, Charlotta Stern, and Jonathan Haidt. "Political Diversity Will Improve Social Psychological Science." *Behavioral and Brain Sciences* 38, no. e130 (2015).

Dunning, David. "False Moral Superiority." In *The Social Psychology of Good and Evil*, edited by Arthur G. Miller. 2nd ed. New York: The Guilford Press, 2016.

Dunning, David, and Nicholas Epley. "Feeling 'Holier than Thou': Are Self-Serving Assessments Produced by Errors in Self- or Social Prediction?" *Journal of Personality and Social Psychology* 79, no. 6 (2000): 861–75.

Fantl, Jeremy. *The Limitations of the Open Mind*. Oxford, New York: Oxford University Press, 2018.

Festinger, Leon. "Cognitive Dissonance." *Scientific American* 207, no. 4 (1962): 93–106.

Finlay, Stephen. "Four Faces of Moral Realism." *Philosophy Compass* 2, no. 6 (2007): 820–49. https://doi.org/10.1111/j.1747-9991.2007.00100.x.

Freiman, Christopher. *Why It's OK to Ignore Politics*. New York: Routledge, 2020.

Gawande, Atul. "Hellhole." *The New Yorker*, March 23, 2009. https://www.newyorker.com/magazine/2009/03/30/hellhole.

Gemes, Ken. "Nietzsche's Critique of Truth." *Philosophy and Phenomenological Research* 52, no. 1 (1992): 47–65.

Gibson, James L., and Joseph L. Sutherland. "Keeping Your Mouth Shut: Spiraling Self-Censorship in the United States," June 1, 2020. SSRN. https://ssrn.com/abstract=3647099.

Gulick, Luther. *Administrative Reflections from World War II*. Tuscaloosa, AL: University of Alabama Press, 1948.

Haidt, Jonathan. *The Righteous Mind*. New York: Vintage, 2012.

Hall, Lars, Petter Johansson, and Thomas Strandberg. "Lifting the Veil of Morality: Choice Blindness and Attitude Reversals on a Self-Transforming Survey." *PLOS One*, 2012. https://doi.org/10.1371/journal.pone.0045457.

Hardin, Garrett. "The Tragedy of the Commons." *Science* 162, no. 3859 (1968): 1243–48.

Hastie, Reid, Steven Penrod, and Nancy Pennington. *Inside the Jury*. Cambridge, MA: Harvard University Press, 1983.

Heron, Woodburn. "The Pathology of Boredom." *Scientific American* 196 (1957): 52–56.

Hightower, Ross, and Lutfus Sayeed. "The Impact of Computer-Mediated Communication Systems on Biased Group Discussion." *Computers in Human Behavior* 11, no. 1 (1995): 33–44.

Hong, Lu, and Scott E. Page. "Groups of Diverse Problem Solvers Can Outperform Groups of High-Ability Problem Solvers." *Proceedings of the National Academy of the Sciences* 101, no. 46 (2004): 16385–89.

Huddleston, Andrew. *Nietzsche on the Decadence and Flourishing of Culture*. New York: Oxford University Press, 2019.

Janis, Irving. *Groupthink*. 2nd ed. Boston, MA: Houghton Mifflin, 1982.

Jenkins, Emily. "Poll: 62% of Americans Say They Have Political Views They're Afraid to Share," July 22, 2020. https://www.cato.org/publications/survey-reports/poll-62-americans-say-they-have-political-views-theyre-afraid-share.

Joshi, Hrishikesh. "What Are the Chances You're Right about Everything? An Epistemic Challenge for Modern Partisanship." *Politics, Philosophy & Economics* 19, no. 1 (2020): 36–61.

Jussim, Lee. *Social Perception and Social Reality: Why Accuracy Dominates Bias and Self-Fulfilling Prophecy*. New York: Oxford University Press, 2012.

Kagan, Shelly. "Do I Make a Difference?" *Philosophy & Public Affairs* 39, no. 2 (2011): 105–41.

Kahan, Dan. "Why We Are Poles Apart on Climate Change." *Nature* 488, no. 255 (2012). https://doi.org/10.1038/488255a.

Kahan, Dan, Ellen Peters, Erica Cantrell Dawson, and Paul Slovic. "Motivated Numeracy and Enlightened Self-Government." *Behavioural Public Policy* 1, no. 1 (2017): 54–86.

Kant, Immanuel. "An Answer to the Question: What Is Enlightenment?" In *Practical Philosophy*, edited by Mary J. Gregor. Cambridge: Cambridge University Press, 1996.

———. "Groundwork of The Metaphysics of Morals." In *Practical Philosophy*, edited by Mary J. Gregor. Cambridge: Cambridge University Press, 1996.

Kelly, Thomas. "Evidence: Fundamental Concepts and the Phenomenal Conception." *Philosophy Compass* 3, no. 5 (2008): 933–55.

Kraut, Richard. *Aristotle on the Human Good*. Princeton, NJ: Princeton University Press, 1989.

Krugman, Paul, and Robin Wells. *Microeconomics*. 3rd ed. New York: Worth Publishers, 2012.

Kuran, Timur. *Private Truths, Public Lies*. Cambridge, MA: Harvard University Press, 1995.

Lackey, Jennifer. "The Duty to Object." *Philosophy and Phenomenological Research*, 2018. https://doi.org/10.1111/phpr.12563.

Latane, Bibb, and Judith Rodin. "A Lady in Distress: Inhibiting Effects of Friends and Strangers on Bystander Intervention." *Journal of Experimental Social Psychology* 5, no. 2 (1969): 189–202.

Lawson, Rebecca. "The Science of Cycology: Failures to Understand How Everyday Objects Work." *Memory & Cognition* 34 (2006): 1667–75.

Leiter, Brian. *Nietzsche on Morality*. 2nd ed. New York: Routledge, 2015.

Longino, Helen. *Science as Social Knowledge*. Princeton, NJ: Princeton University Press, 1990.

Loury, Glenn. "Self-Censorship in Public Discourse." *Rationality and Society* 6, no. 4 (1994): 428–61.

Mankiw, N. Gregory. *Principles of Economics*. 7th ed. Stamford, CT: Cengage Learning, 2014.

Marques, José M., Vincent Y. Yzerbyt, and Jacques-Philippe Leyens. "The 'Black Sheep Effect': Extremity of Judgments towards Ingroup Members as a Function of Group Identification." *European Journal of Social Psychology* 18, no. 1 (January 1, 1988): 1–16. https://doi.org/10.1002/ejsp.2420180102.

Maudlin, Tim. *Philosophy of Physics: Quantum Theory*. Princeton, NJ: Princeton University Press, 2019.

———. *Philosophy of Physics: Space and Time*. Princeton, NJ: Princeton University Press, 2012.

Mercier, Hugo, and Dan Sperber. *The Enigma of Reason*. Cambridge, MA: Harvard University Press, 2017.

Mill, John Stuart. *On Liberty and Other Essays*. Edited by John Gray. Oxford, New York: Oxford University Press, 2008.

Mueller, Dennis C. *Public Choice III*. New York: Cambridge University Press, 2003.

Mynatt, Clifford, Michael Doherty, and Ryan Tweney. "Confirmation Bias in a Simulated Research Environment: An Experimental Study of Scientific Inference." *Quarterly Journal of Experimental Psychology* 29, no. 1 (1977): 85–95.

Nefsky, Julia. "How You Can Help, without Making a Difference." *Philosophical Studies* 174 (2017): 2743–67.

Nehamas, Alexander. *Nietzsche: Life as Literature*. Cambridge, MA: Harvard University Press, 1985.

Nietzsche, Friedrich. "The Antichrist." In *The Portable Nietzsche*, translated by Walter Kaufmann. New York: Penguin Books, 1954.

———. *Beyond Good and Evil*. Translated by Walter Kaufmann. New York: Random House, 1966.

———. "The Dawn." In *The Portable Nietzsche*, translated by Walter Kaufmann. New York: Penguin Books, 1954.

———. "Ecce Homo." In *On the Genealogy of Morals and Ecce Homo*, edited by Walter Kaufmann, Reissue edition. New York: Vintage, 1989.

———. *The Gay Science*. Translated by Walter Kaufmann. New York: Random House, 1974.

———. "Human, All-Too-Human." In *The Portable Nietzsche*, translated by Walter Kaufmann. New York: Penguin Books, 1954.

———. "On the Genealogy of Morals." In *On the Genealogy of Morals and Ecce Homo*, edited by Walter Kaufmann, Reissue edition. New York: Vintage, 1989.

———. "Schopenhauer as Educator." In *Untimely Meditations*, edited by Daniel Breazeale, translated by R.J. Hollingdale. Cambridge, UK: Cambridge University Press, 1997.

———. "Thus Spoke Zarathustra." In *The Portable Nietzsche*, translated by Walter Kaufmann. New York: Penguin Books, 1954.

———. "Twilight of the Idols." In *The Portable Nietzsche*, translated by Walter Kaufmann. New York: Penguin Books, 1954.

Noelle-Neumann, Elisabeth. *The Spiral of Silence*. Chicago, IL: University of Chicago Press, 1984.

———. "The Spiral of Silence: A Theory of Public Opinion." *Journal of Communication* 24, no. 2 (June 1, 1974): 43–51. https://doi.org/10.1111/j.1460-2466.1974.tb00367.x.

Orwell, George. 1984. Mass Market Paperback. New York: Signet Classics, 1961.

Ostrom, Elinor. "Collective Action and the Evolution of Social Norms." *Journal of Economic Perspectives* 14, no. 3 (2000): 137–58.

Pinker, Steven. *The Blank Slate*. New York: Penguin Books, 2002.

Pipes, Richard. *Communism: A History*. New York: Random House, 2001.

Plato. "Apology." In *Plato: Complete Works*, edited by John Cooper. Indianapolis, IN: Hackett Publishing, 1997.

Reginster, Bernard. *The Affirmation of Life*. Cambridge, MA: Harvard University Press, 2006.

Ridley, Aaron. *Nietzsche's Conscience*. Ithaca, NY: Cornell University Press, 1998.

Ross, W.D. *The Right and the Good*. Oxford: Oxford University Press, 1930.

Rozenblit, Leonid, and Frank Keil. "The Misunderstood Limits of Folk Science: An Illusion of Explanatory Depth." *Cognitive Science* 26, no. 5 (2002): 521–62.

Russell, Bertrand. "The Best Answer to Fanaticism—Liberalism." *The New York Times Magazine*, December 16, 1951. https://www.nytimes.com/1951/12/16/archives/the-best-answer-to-fanaticismliberalism-its-calm-search-for-truth.html.

————. "Free Thought and Official Propaganda." Watts & Co., 1922. https://www.gutenberg.org/files/44932/44932-h/44932-h.htm.

Scheffler, Samuel. *Death and the Afterlife*. The Berkeley Tanner Lectures. New York: Oxford University Press, 2016.

Shi, Feng, Mish Teplitskiy, Eamon Duede, and James A Evans. "The Wisdom of Polarized Crowds." *Nature Human Behavior* 3 (2019): 329–36.

Shiffrin, Seana. *Speech Matters: On Lying, Morality, and the Law*. Princeton, NJ: Princeton University Press, 2014.

Silver, David, Julian Schrittwieser, Karen Simonyan, Ioannis Antonoglou, Aja Huang, Arthur Guez, Thomas Hubert, et al. "Mastering the Game of Go without Human Knowledge." *Nature* 550, no. 7676 (October 1, 2017): 354–59. https://doi.org/10.1038/nature24270.

Simler, Kevin, and Robin Hanson. *The Elephant in the Brain*. New York: Oxford University Press, 2018.

Sloman, Steven A., and Philip Fernbach. *The Knowledge Illusion: Why We Never Think Alone*. New York: Riverhead Books, 2017.

Smith, Adam. *An Inquiry into the Nature and Causes of the Wealth of Nations*. 3rd ed (1871). London: Alex Murray & Son, 1776.

Stasser, Garold, Susanne Abele, and Sandra Vaughan Parsons. "Information Flow and Influence in Collective Choice." *Group Processes & Intergroup Relations* 15, no. 5 (2012): 619–35.

Stasser, Garold, and William Titus. "Hidden Profiles: A Brief History." *Psychological Inquiry* 14, no. 3/4 (2003): 304–13.

————. "Pooling of Unshared Information in Group Decision Making: Biased Information Sampling During Discussion." *Journal of Personality and Social Psychology* 48, no. 6 (1985): 1467–78.

Sunstein, Cass. *Conformity*. New York: New York University Press, 2019.

Sunstein, Cass, and Reid Hastie. *Wiser: Getting Beyond Groupthink to Make Groups Smarter*. Boston, MA: Harvard Business Review Press, 2015.

Sunstein, Cass, Reid Hastie, and David Schkade. "What Happened on Deliberation Day?" *95 California Law Review* 915 (2007).

Taber, Charles, and Milton Lodge. "Motivated Skepticism in the Evaluation of Political Beliefs." *American Journal of Political Science* 50, no. 3 (2006): 755–69.

Tappin, Ben, and Ryan McKay. "The Illusion of Moral Superiority." *Social Psychological and Personality Science* 8, no. 6 (2017): 623–31.

Thomson, Judith Jarvis. *Normativity*. Chicago, IL: Open Court, 2008.

Tosi, Justin, and Brandon Warmke. *Grandstanding: The Use and Abuse of Moral Talk.* New York: Oxford University Press, 2020.

Trivers, Robert. *The Folly of Fools: The Logic of Deceit and Self-Deception in Human Life.* New York: Basic Books, 2011.

Trouche, Emmanuel, Petter Johansson, Lars Hall, and Hugo Mercier. "The Selective Laziness of Reasoning." *Cognitive Science* 40, no. 8 (2016): 2122–36.

Wason, Peter. "Reasoning about a Rule." *Quarterly Journal of Experimental Psychology* 20, no. 3 (1968): 273–81.

West, Richard F., Russell J. Meserve, and Keith E. Stanovich. "Cognitive Sophistication Does Not Attenuate the Bias Blind Spot." *Journal of Personality and Social Psychology* 103, no. 3 (2012): 506–19.

Willer, Robb, Ko Kuwabara, and Michael W. Macy. "The False Enforcement of Unpopular Norms." *American Journal of Sociology* 115, no. 2 (2009): 451–90.

Wootton, David. *Galileo: Watcher of the Skies.* New Haven, CT: Yale University Press, 2010.

Index

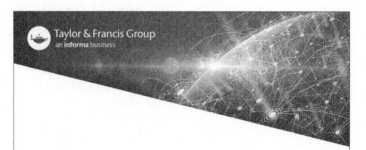